Contributing Authors
Karen Bagby, M. Ed.
Leonard J. Basile, M. Ed.
Jodi McClay, M.A.
Annette Hauenstein Wallace

Editor
Marsha Kearns

Editorial Manager
Ina Massler Levin, M.A.

Editor in Chief
Sharon Coan, M.S. Ed.

Illustrator
Howard Chaney

Cover Artists
Sue Fullam
Mark Kazlauskas

Associate Designer
Denise Bauer

Creative Director
Elayne Roberts

Imaging
Ralph Olmedo, Jr.
Alfred Lau
James Edward Grace

Product Manager
Phil Garcia

Publisher
Mary D. Smith, M.S. Ed.

HOW TO
Learning Centers
IN THE CLASSROOM

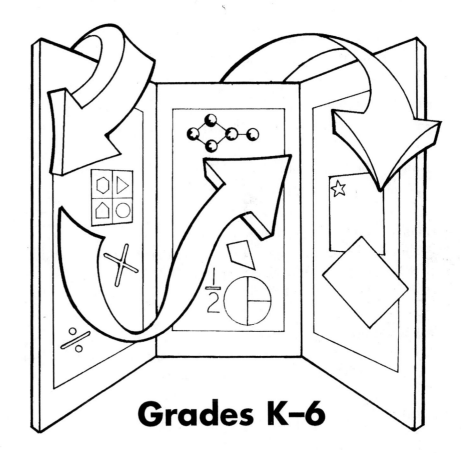

Grades K–6

Written and Compiled by

Dona Rice

Teacher
Created
Resources

Teacher Created Resources, Inc.
6421 Industry Way
Westminster, CA 92683
www.teachercreated.com
©*1996 Teacher Created Resources, Inc.*
Reprinted, 2006
Made in U.S.A.
ISBN-13: 978-1-57690-037-6
ISBN-10: 1-57690-037-1

Table of Contents

Table of Contents *(cont.)*

Introduction

Teachers understand and strive to accommodate the fact that their students have different learning styles and ability levels among the various curriculum areas. One way teachers can provide students the opportunity to work at their own pace in a manner most appropriate to their personal learning style is to establish classroom learning centers. Learning centers maximize flexibility in the classroom, which in turn helps minimize disruption.

Even though all students must learn the same skills, learning centers provide opportunities for students to work at their own paces and ability levels, without the accompanying boredom often experienced by the advanced learner or the frustration felt by the learner who needs more time and practice. Learning for everyone becomes what learning is intended to be—exciting and motivating.

Students may spend as much or as little time as they need to acquire knowledge or master a skill without feeling rushed, bored, or inadequate. The ability of students to move from center to center helps ensure that they internalize learning in the best way for them individually rather than having to adapt to a presentation geared for the "average" student.

With the use of learning centers, classrooms become less teacher-directed and more student-centered. As students' personal power grows, they are motivated to experiment with acquiring knowledge and understanding in the ways most natural and interesting for them. The real-life skills that are naturally acquired through the use of centers—things such as time management, cooperation, responsibility, and flexibility—are precisely the skills that every student will need as he or she moves ever closer to becoming part of the adult world.

What does a learning center–based classroom look like? What will you need for each center? How can you teach students to use the centers easily and effectively? What is the best way to assess learning? *How to Manage Learning Centers in the Classroom* is a comprehensive guide that answers those questions and more. In it you will find unique and innovative suggestions, diagrams, and tools that show you exactly how you can establish, organize, and effectively use learning centers in Grades K–6. Within the framework provided, you can easily modify the techniques and suggestions for your particular classroom and class's needs.

This book is designed to help teachers and students make the most of their shared school experience and to further their common goal of ensuring that each student realize his or her potential for learning and growing. Discover for yourself how the use of centers can enhance your teaching and your students' learning every day.

Learning Centers Management Model

This model for centers management (pages 5–26) is designed to reinforce all areas of the curriculum and to help students internalize learning at their own levels. Additionally, it offers opportunities to challenge each student in a nonthreatening environment. You may wish to gather these materials to have on hand as you follow the management model presented. Or you may wish to read the whole book to see which suggestions work best for you. Either way, the materials and forms you need are page-referenced throughout in the appropriate places to make it easy for you to assemble what you need for your centers-based classroom.

Materials:

- 7 tubs about 10" x 12" x 6" (25 cm x 30 cm x 15 cm)
- approximately 70 wooden clothespins
- self-adhesive Velcro® ¹/₂" x 36" (1.5 cm x 90 cm)
- tagboard
- supplies baskets about 6" x 6" (15 cm x 15 cm)
- student sets of pencils, crayons, scissors, and glue
- paint
- paintbrush
- laminating machine
- locator and tub cards
- pocket folders (approximately 6 each of red, orange, yellow, green, and blue)
- yarn or string
- stapler
- push pins or tape
- glue
- bell, buzzer, or alarm
- cassette or compact disc player
- nature sounds or other peaceful music
- clean-up music
- Centers Groups chart
- Centers Contracts

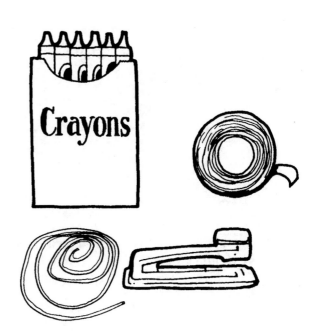

Getting Organized

The sooner you implement your learning center plan the smoother your classroom will begin to run. What appears unimaginable when you consider the large picture seems manageable when you consider each step in order and understand how it fits into the overall setup and functioning of your classroom. You need to know what to do and what your classroom will look like before students come to the first day of school. The first four weeks of the Centers program will focus on training students in how to effectively use the centers, their folders and contracts, and their time. Use this management model as a guideline for creating your own plan.

Preplanning for the Students

1. Assign each student a number that will be his or hers for the school year. You may wish to use the same numbers as the list in your grade book (alphabetically) or assign numbers randomly. Be sure to make a permanent record of the numbers and keep it handy.

2. Color code the days of the week: Monday = red, Tuesday = orange, Wednesday = yellow, Thursday = green, Friday = blue. You may wish to create a Centers bulletin board upon which you can make and display a chart showing the day/color code as well as other information specific to using learning centers.

3. Divide the class into five groups. Assign each student a group and each group a contract start day (Monday through Friday).

4. Reproduce a Centers Groups chart (page 8). Write the students' names and numbers in the appropriate column for their contract start day. Display the chart on your Centers bulletin board.

5. To create a relaxing, yet stimulating environment during Centers time, gather a selection of background music such as nature tapes to play.

6. Choose a sound, such as a bell or buzzer, as a warning to the class that Centers time is almost over and that they have two minutes to finish their center activities.

7. Select another piece of music, about three minutes long, that will signal clean-up time. Two minutes after sounding the warning, play this selection as a cue for students to have the room cleaned up and be seated at their own desks by the time the music ends.

Getting Organized *(cont.)*

Preparing for the Centers

Each learning center will have a large color/shape-coded sign designating the center, a color/shape-coded plastic tub or area for the activities, and color-coded clothespins. In addition, providing each group of student desks (or tables) with a smaller basket that can hold classroom supplies eliminates the need for students to carry supplies with them as they move around the room during Centers time. These baskets can also be permanently stationed on each group of desks (or tables) to be used throughout the school day for other activities.

1. Determine and name the learning centers you want, and code each with a shape, such as Meet with Teacher = rectangle, Reading = heart, Writing = oval, etc. Content area centers may include listening, math, science, social studies, computers, art, and music.

2. Make and display on your Centers bulletin board a name/shape/color = code key of the learning centers. (You may wish to use a copy of the Centers Contract (page 287) for this by coloring the shapes and writing the names of the learning centers on the appropriate lines.)

3. Reproduce pages 9–20. Paint each shape a different color, cut it out, and laminate it onto a 12" x 12" (30 cm x 30 cm) square of poster board to hang over its appropriate center. (You may want to make the signs double sided.)

4. Gather 5-7 (50-70 spring-clip wooden clothespins for each center and paint them the same color as the center's shape color. Meet with Teacher center does not require any clothespins. The teacher will seek out the students one on one and may choose to review their work at the teacher's desk or at the center that the student is currently working at. After the clothespins are painted attach enough clothespins to the signs and tub cards. The amount of clothespins to be used per center will be determined by the number of spaces available at each center, usually 4-6.

5. Gather as many plastic tubs 10" x 12" x 6" (25 cm x 30 cm x 15 cm) as you have designated learning centers. You may not need tubs for the Library, Computer, Listening, Games, and Meet with Teacher centers, instead you will use laminated signs that can be found on pages 244-265.

6. Reproduce pages 21–22 and paint the small shapes to correspond to each center's color. Cut out the shapes and laminate them to a white, unlined 4" x 6" (10.54 cm x 15 cm) index card. Affix each one to the outside of a tub using self-adhesive Velcro strips.

7. Laminate a piece of tagboard 6" x 9" (15 cm x 22.5 cm) for each tub. This will be the clothespin holder for the center's tubs. Affix each one to the inside of a tub using self-adhesive Velcro® strips.

8. Gather six smaller plastic tubs or baskets to be permanently stationed at each group of desks (or tables). Provide enough supplies in each basket for the maximum number of students in the group. Each basket should contain scissors, glue, crayons, and pencils.

Centers Groups

Student #	Monday (red)	Student #	Tuesday (orange)	Student #	Wednesday (yellow)	Student #	Thursday (green)	Student #	Friday (blue)

8

Center Locator Cards

Center Locator Cards (cont.)

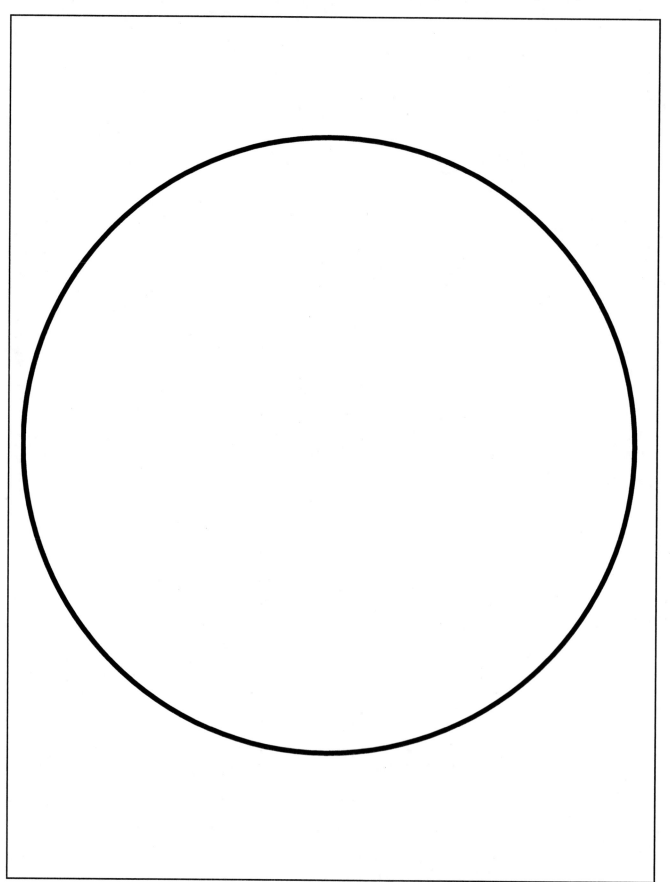

Center Locator Cards *(cont.)*

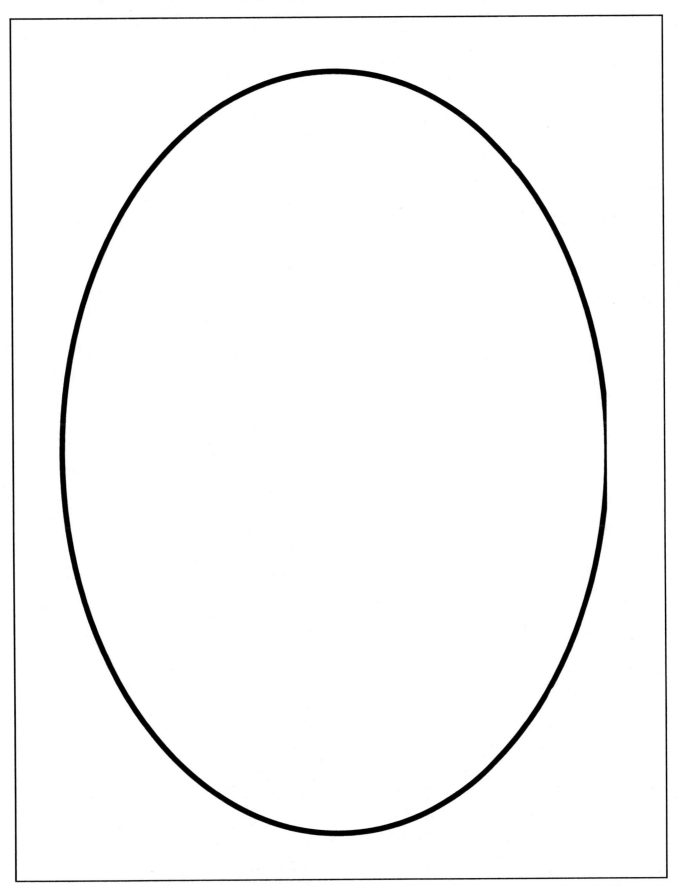

Center Locator Cards (cont.)

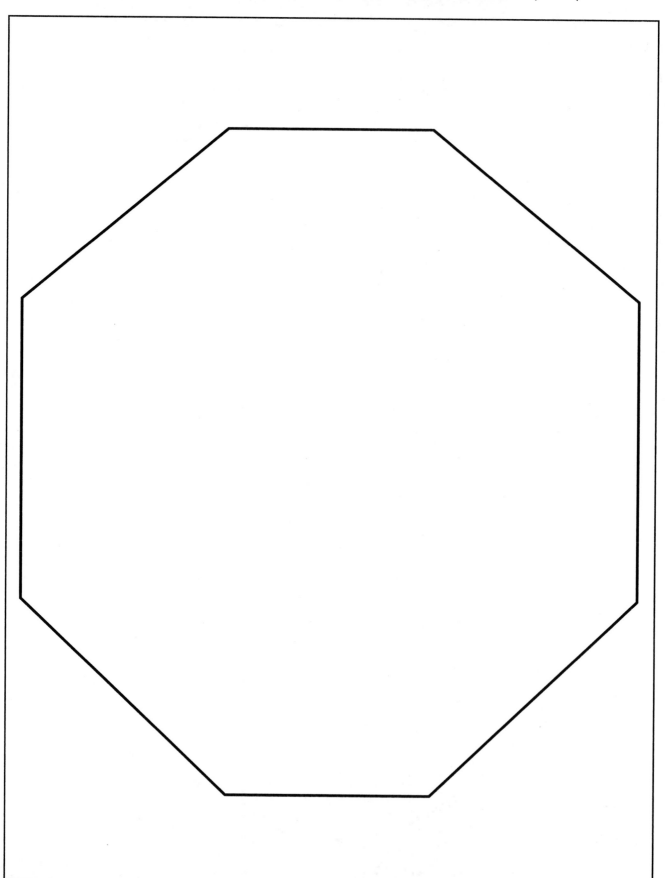

Center Locator Cards (cont.)

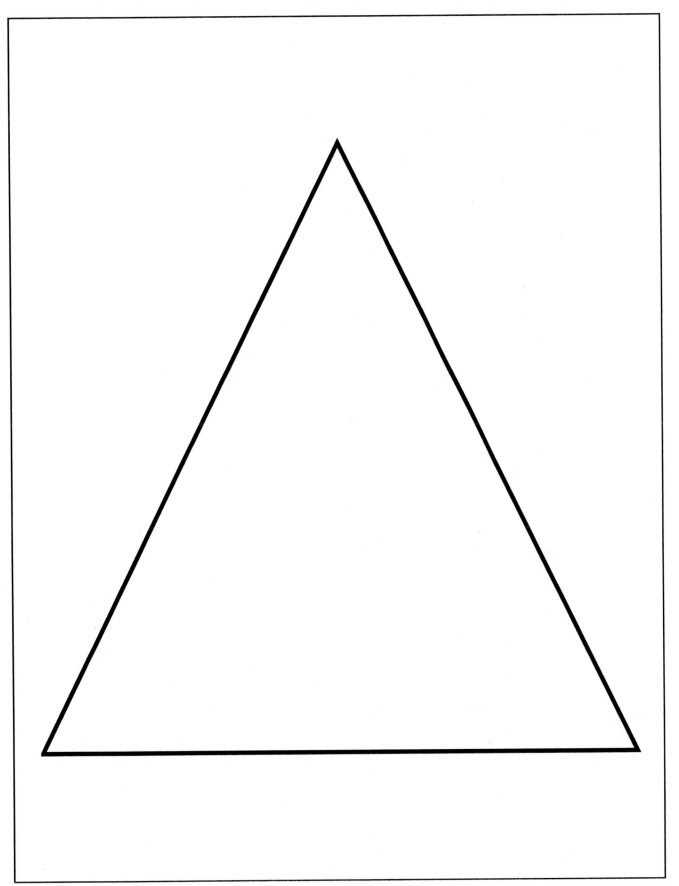

Center Locator Cards (cont.)

Center Locator Cards (cont.)

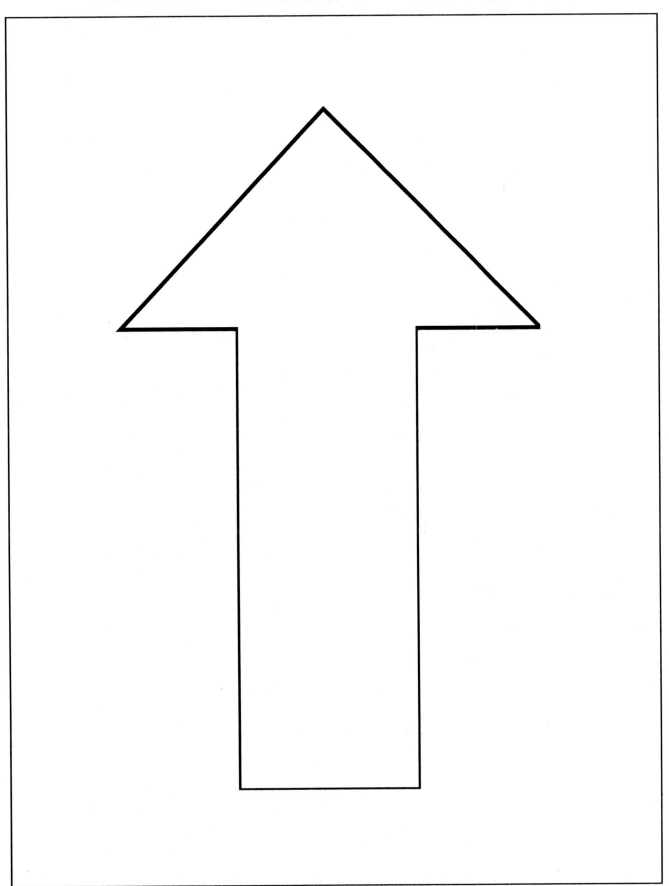

Center Locator Cards (cont.)

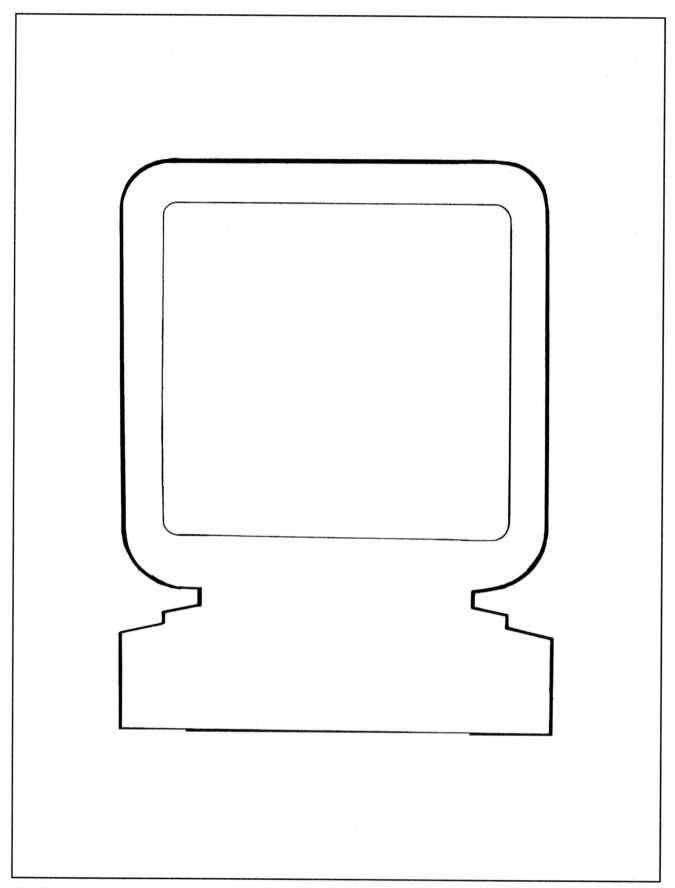

Center Locator Cards *(cont.)*

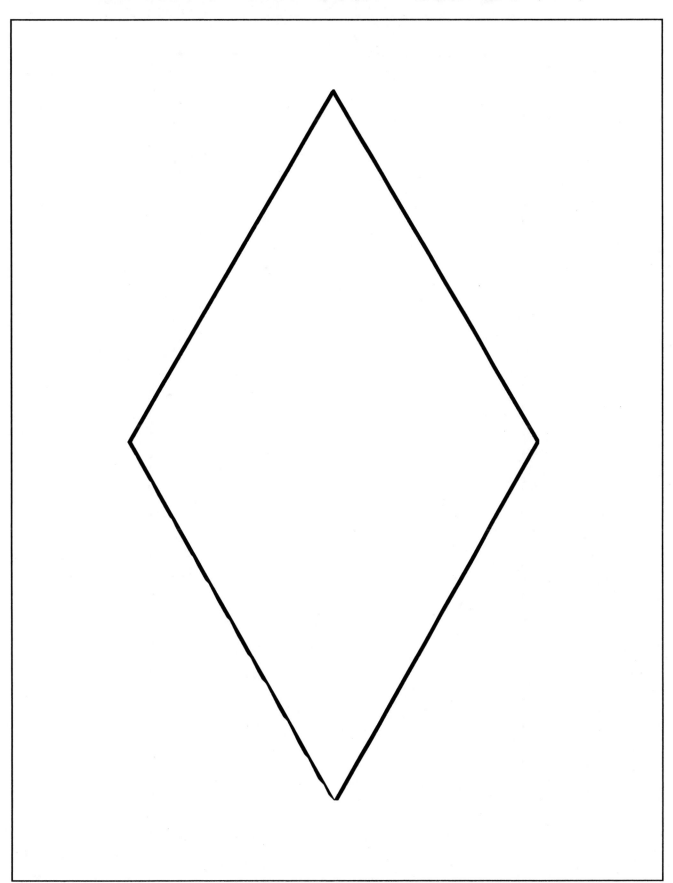

Center Locator Cards *(cont.)*

Center Locator Cards (cont.)

Center Locator Cards *(cont.)*

Tub Cards

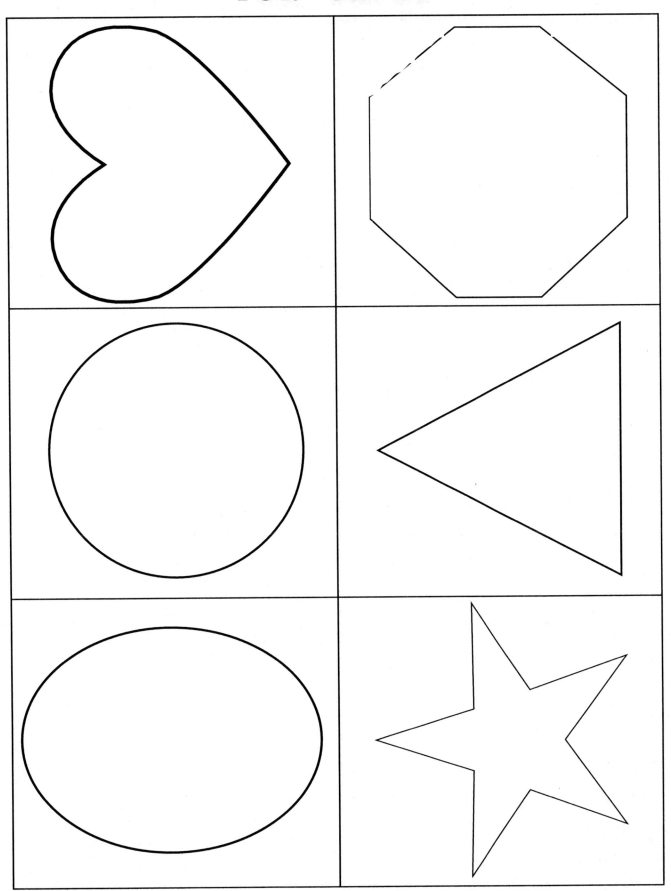

Tub Cards (cont.)

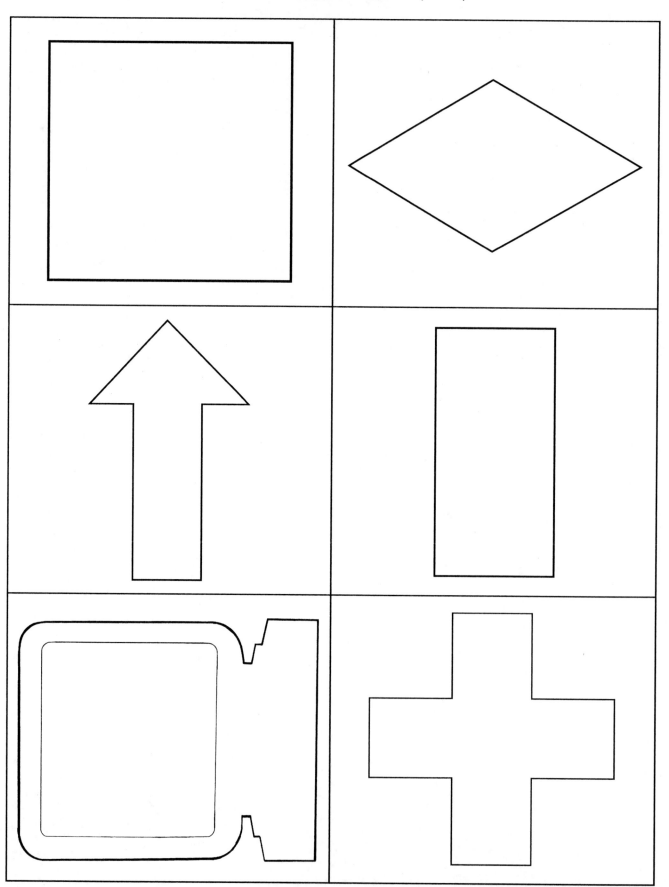

Classroom Arrangement

An organized classroom management system will provide you and your students with a more effective learning environment. Arranging the classroom is extremely important. In this model, student desks are arranged into six groups in the middle of the classroom. Other learning centers are stationed around the perimeter of the room.

Model Map

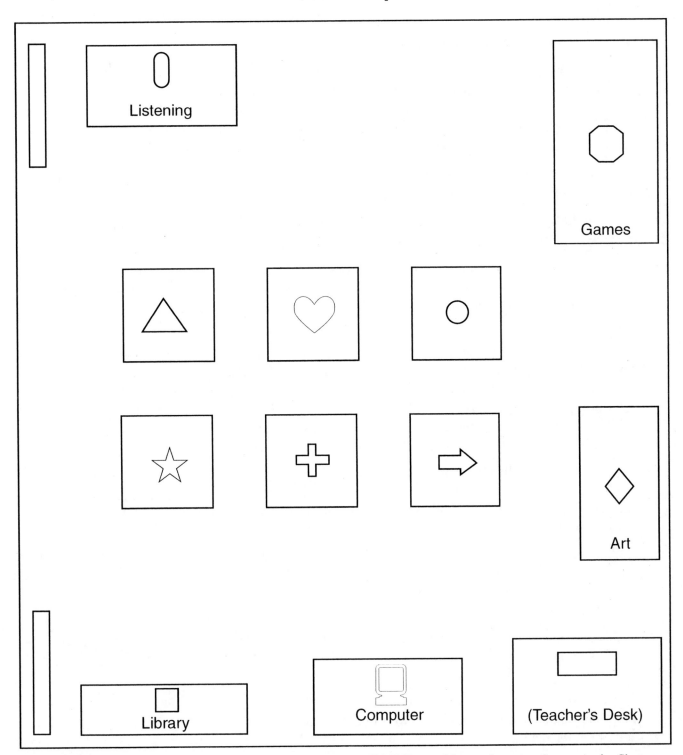

Getting Started

The first four weeks of the program focus on training students in how to use the learning centers, their folders, and the designated Centers time. During this time, little will be spent on academic objectives. After the program is in place, the objective of the activities will become more academic. After the first day you will introduce and open another new center daily until all of the centers are open. When all of the centers are open, you will change the activities in at least one center and no more than three centers every day. Each center is designed to last on the average of five days. This allows each of the students the opportunity to do all of the activities.

Before the First Day of School

1. Make sure your classroom is arranged (see pages 23), each center area is designated by a shape, centers tubs prepared and placed on an accessible shelf, the signs (computer, games, library, and listening) are located around the perimeter of the room, the supply baskets prepared and placed at each group (student desks). These centers can have math manipulatives or puzzles to be used for free exploration, the seventh center will be located at the Art center for drawing.

2. Enlarge, color, laminate, and display on the Centers bulletin board the Rules for Using Learning Centers (page 63).

Week 1—Objective: To teach students how to move about the classroom and use the Centers and Centers time

1. Begin using the centers on the first day of school by opening seven centers. The first six centers are to be stationed at each group (student desks). These centers can have math manipulatives or puzzles to be used for free exploration, the seventh center will be located at the Art center for drawing.

2. Introduce the concept of centers and Centers time. Point out to the class the centers, the Centers bulletin board, the Centers Groups chart, their student numbers, and the color/shape codes. Show students the centers tubs and baskets and tell them that the weekly group leaders, (each group has their group leader who rotates weekly) each day will be responsible for carrying the appropriate tub to their table. For example if a student is the group's leader in the circle's group, he or she will get the tub with the circle shape on it and place it on the desks in the circle group.

3. Tell the class that when it is Centers time, they will each go to a center, attach a clothespin to their clothing, and work at the activity that is in the tub. If the center they choose does not have a clothespin available it means the center is full and the student must go to another center.

4. Explain to students that when they are finished at a center, they should clean their area (including the floor, if necessary), put their clothespins back, push their chairs in, and go quietly to another center.

5. Tell students they will have one hour for Centers time. Play the music you have chosen as background music and tell students that when they hear it, they will continue working at centers.

6. Introduce students to the warning sound. Tell them that when they hear that sound, they will have two minutes to complete the activity at the center.

Getting Started (cont.)

Week 1 (cont.)

7. Play a portion of the clean-up music selection only on the first day and tell students that when they hear it they must have the room cleaned and be back in their seats by the time the music ends.

8. Now it is time to begin centers. Explain the activities in the tubs. Have the designated group leaders get the tubs to be placed on their group's table. Excuse the students to attend the centers. Using the Centers Group chart, read the names of the student in each color (day) group. If you begin on Monday, (red day) call the orange group to go to the center of their choice, followed by the yellow group, green, blue, and finally the red group. This order is explained in week 4.

9. Play the background music and circulate around the room making sure the students understand how to use the centers and move among them.

10. After an hour, signal the warning and remind students to finish with their activities. After two minutes play the clean-up music and remind students to clean up the centers and be seated at their desks before the music ends.

Week 2—Objective: To teach students how to use their folders during Centers time

Have available for each student a pocket folder in his/her group's color (day). For example, if a student's contract start day is Monday, his or her pocket folder will be red. If the start day is Tuesday, the folder will be orange, etc.

1. Before beginning Centers time, tell students that they will begin to carry folders with them during Centers.

2. If you start on a Monday, hand out a red pocket folder to all students in the red group. Their name and number should already be written on the front of the pocket folder. Let the other students know that they will receive their colored folders on their group's contract start day.

3. Explain to the Monday (red) group the rules for using folders (as the rest of the class listens):

   1. Take your folder to every center.   3. Handle your papers and folders with care.

   2. Put all your papers in your folder.   4. Do not take your folders home.

You may wish to display these rules on your Centers bulletin board.

4. Begin Centers time and closely monitor the red group students as they use the centers, reminding them to put their papers into their folders. After centers have the Monday group keep their folders in their desks to use during the next Centers time.

5. Every day follow the same teaching procedure with a new group. Beginning on the third week each color group will receive their pocket folder cleaned out with a new prepared Centers Contract in it. Use the following procedure to accomplish this.

On the fifth day (or Friday) of the second week during clean-up time have the red group turn in their folders to have their work evaluated so they may begin with an empty folder and a new contract beginning the third week. On Monday have the orange group turn in their folders during clean-up, so they may begin with a clean folder an a new Centers Contract on Tuesday. Continue this process daily. On Tuesday, the yellow group, Wednesday—green group, Thursday—blue group, again on Friday the red group will turn in their folders. This process should cycle throughout the remainder of the school year.

Getting Started *(cont.)*

Week 3—Objective: To teach students how to use their Centers Contract

Reproduce a copy of the Centers Contract (page 287) to create a master contract. Write the center names next to the corresponding shape. Reproduce a copy of the master contract for each student.

1. Before beginning Centers time, tell the class that they will begin using a Centers Contract to make sure they attend and complete the activities in all the centers.

2. Tell students they will have five school days to complete a contract.

3. On Monday of the third week, hand out the red pocket folders with the Centers Contracts inside. The student's name and number should already be filled out. Explain how to use it (as the rest of the class listens). During centers watch this group closely to ensure their success in this program. Throughout the remainder of this week you will continue this same procedure. Closely monitor the group that has a new contract to ensure they understand the program. While closely monitoring the new group, check the previous groups(s) to ensure that they too are following the program.

   a. Every five days you will get a new contract.

   b. Write your name, student number, and start date on the contract.

   c. During Centers time, you will color in the first column of bubbles as you move from center to center. No matter what your group's start day (Monday = red, etc.), you will color the bubbles according to the day you attend the center. For example, if you are in the Friday (blue) group, you will have a blue folder. But for the centers you attend on Monday, you will color the bubbles red. The center bubbles you visit on Tuesday will be orange, and so on. (Point out the key on the contract as a reminder.)

   d. If you finish your whole column of bubbles before the five days are up, you may revisit the centers and use the second column of bubbles. You may only visit a center a second time if you have completed your first column of bubbles and have attended each center, or you need to complete a center that was left incomplete the day before during due to clean-up time.

   e. After five days, you will meet with me. I will check your contracts and help you plan your Centers time and prepare your contract for the next five days.

Week 4—Objective: To teach students how their weekly Centers work will be evaluated and to introduce the next week's contract

Reproduce a copy of the Request for Supplies (page 74) for each student. Have students take it home to their parents, along with their first completed Centers Contract.

1. On Monday during Centers time introduce any new centers. Have the group leaders get the tubs. When excusing students to centers begin with the orange group. This enables them to go to any center first, allowing them to complete their contracts in case a center that hasn't been done is available. The yellow group will be excused second followed by the green, blue, and finally the red group. On Tuesday, excuse the yellow group first followed by the green group, blue, red, and finally the orange group. Throughout the remainder of the week and every week thereafter, follow the same rotation.

2. Encourage students to complete at least three centers per day which allows them to complete their contracts successfully.

3. During conference time, review the student's work and provide feedback. Write a comment for his or her parent on the contract sheet. Staple the contract to the front of his or her papers and send the stack home for parent review. Ask that the contract be returned on the following day with a parent's signature.

Setting Up Centers

Centers need to be designed so that students are able to complete the activities with little or no assistance from an adult. Some teachers use volunteers or older students to monitor and help students working at centers; other teachers use centers to also teach responsibility and independence and expect students to complete most of the activities on their own.

You can set up a center for nearly any subject and make the activities part of the main lesson or as lesson extensions (i.e. science investigations where students have time to examine something more in depth). Centers can be highly structured or as open as putting together jigsaw puzzles. Use your imagination and creativity to set up centers that will be exciting, challenging, and interesting and provide students important opportunities to work individually, to be responsible for completing assignments on their own, and to make choices.

Things to Keep in Mind When Setting Up Centers

1. Have some form of symbolic directions for students (and student helpers) to easily follow even though you may have explained things orally. These symbols will help students who are not yet reading or who do not listen well. Symbols and signs for duplication can be found on pages 243–268.

cut   paste   write

2. Decorate centers so that they are inviting to students. Use the bottom part of a bulletin board, a chart taped to a wall, a wooden stand, or a cardboard carrel to post directions.

Things to Keep in Mind (cont.)

3. Be sure the center has all the materials that students will need so they will not have to interrupt their work to find something. A box, basket, or tub will remind students where to put the center's supplies when they are finished or when time is up.

Name: _____	
Color, Cut, Paste	
Red Apple	
Yellow Banana	
Brown Bread	
Blue Ball	

4. Provide a way for students to record which centers they have completed. Below is a sample. You may wish to reproduce page 47 for each student to use. This form has a column for you or a helper to check that the work was completed. This column could also be used to indicate the student's success level for that work, i.e., amount completed or accuracy of work.

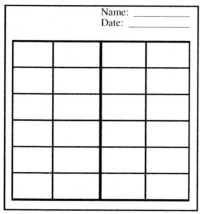

Name: _____
Date: _____

5. Design a method for students to check their own work at centers whenever possible.

6. Decide how you want students to use the centers. Options include:

   a. Centers may be used by students whenever they finish their regular assignment.

   b. Students may work at centers during an assigned time while you work with groups on enrichment or reteaching.

   c. You may establish a regular daily Centers time when all students work at center activities.

7. Setting up enough activities for a week (or longer) will free you from continually thinking about setting up more centers. Many times center activities relate to classroom instruction, but all centers need not relate to a specific area of study.

8. To make any classroom space a center area, make and use carrels (page 29).

Carrels

One of the easiest ways to set up centers is with a carrel. Follow these directions to make them simply and inexpensively.

Materials:

- large, sturdy cardboard box
- wrapping paper, shelf paper, or construction paper
- wide book-binding tape (option: masking tape or duct tape)
- clear tape
- scissors

Directions:

1. Cut out the bottom and two long sides of the cardboard box.
2. Using clear tape, cover each rectangle completely in wrapping paper, shelf paper, or construction paper.
3. Lay the rectangles vertically next to one another, with the largest section in the middle. Leave about $1/2$" (1.25 cm) between each rectangle.
4. Create hinges by taping the rectangles together with book-binding tape. (Duct or masking tape work but are not as attractive.) Tape the rectangles together in front and in back so that all the stickiness is covered.
5. Bend the hinges and place the carrel on a desk or table.

Note: If you make mobile centers (page 31), carrels can be used directly at the students' desks. This is especially helpful when you have limited classroom space.

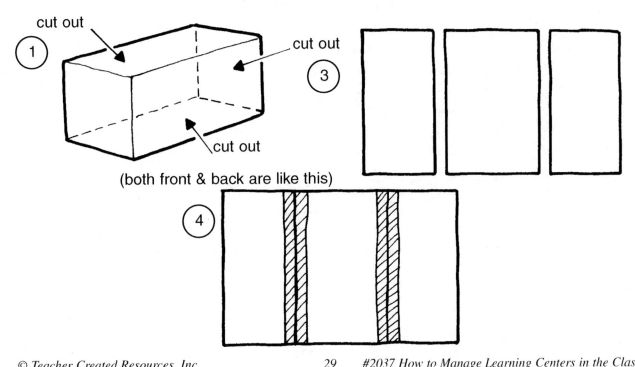

Megacenters

In multi-age or multi-level classrooms, it may prove useful to create megacenters. A megacenter is a grouping of centers offering a variety of activities at different levels. The megacenter structure enables students to work in depth on self-initiated projects.

Students sign up for or are assigned to a megacenter for a long period of time, usually an hour or more. If a student finishes a project quickly, he or she may move to other enticing activities to fill the time allotted. This prevents students from wandering around the classroom and bothering others. Choice increases motivation.

Here are some suggestions for megacenter groupings:

- Home centers blend well with dramatic play, puppetry, and library centers.

- Art and publishing are a natural combination. Students may become authors and illustrators by creating a complete book. This megacenter should include a table, art supplies, and some easels. (Tabletop easels can be used to save space.) In addition, students should have access to a nearby sink to make cleaning up easier.

- Computers and research go well together. You may also choose to locate the main library in this center instead of the Drama Center. To provide quiet alternative activities, include puzzles, pegboards, parquetry, and other manipulatives in this megacenter.

- A table located between the Research Center and the Reading/Skills Center can serve both centers.

- A theme center can also be the science and/or social studies center.

Stationary and Mobile Centers

Learning centers can be set up in a variety of ways. Be sure the setup option you choose is compatible with your classroom space and teaching style. If you have the room and your centers can be stationary, be sure that each center has space for storage (baskets, shelves, tubs, drawers) and an area for posting directions, samples, or other pertinent information.

If you use mobile centers, it is best to use large plastic tubs with lids. Tubs can hold all necessary materials for the center and can be easily carried to desks and work tables when needed. Student directions, sample work, and other information can be taped to the inside of the tub lid.

Writing Center

In both cases, be sure that the materials you use are durable. Use heavy paper and laminate the materials wherever possible. This will not only preserve your supplies, but it will make them easier for the students to use.

Labeling is key when setting up centers. Designate all center areas with signs. Also label the materials and information used in each center. This takes more effort up front, but everyone benefits in the long run—students move more smoothly and quickly down the road of independent learning, and you will not have to repeatedly give directions or answer questions.

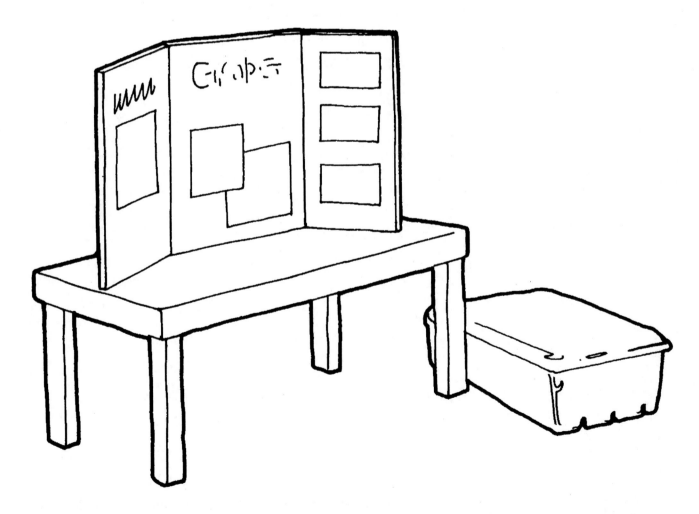

Arranging the Classroom

Look at the examples of classroom maps and possible learning center arrangements provided. Then use the classroom map on page 34 and the furniture icons on page 35 to work out the best arrangement for your class.

Sample Classroom Map #1

Front

Reading Table		Display Table
Center	X X X X X X X X	
Center	X X X X X X X X	
Center	X X X X X X X X	
Center	X X X X X X X X	
Center		Teacher's Desk
Center		
Library	Reading Table	Center Center
		Coat Closet

Arranging the Classroom *(cont.)*

Sample Classroom Map #2

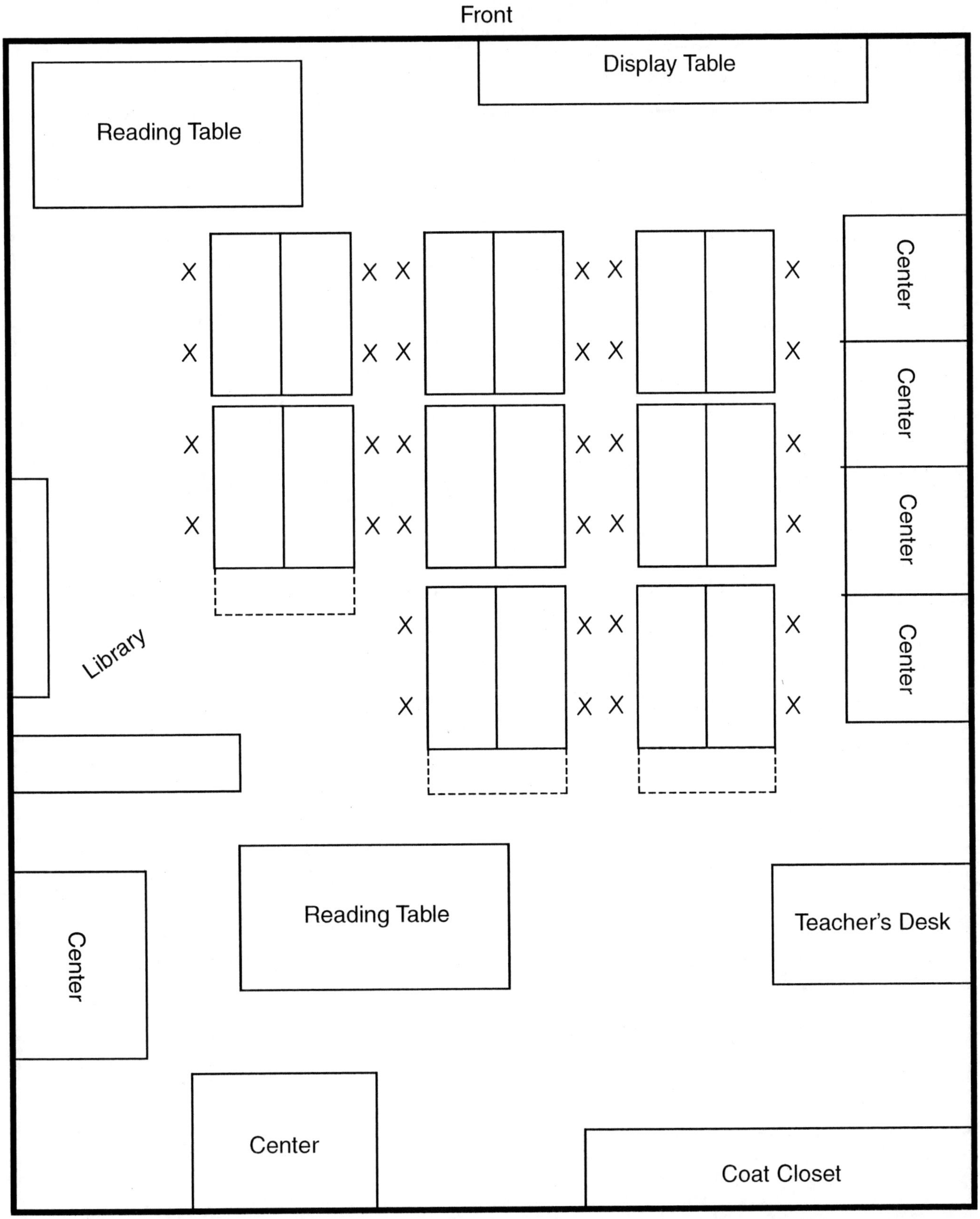

Front

Display Table

Reading Table

Center

Center

Center

Center

Library

Center

Reading Table

Teacher's Desk

Center

Center

Coat Closet

Arranging the Classroom (cont.)

Your Classroom Map

Reproduce the rectangle below. On your classroom map, designate the front of your room. Then show where the doors, windows, bulletin boards, chalkboards, and electrical outlets are in the room. Reproduce page 35, cut out the "furniture" icons, and place them on your classroom map until you find the best arrangement for your room.

Arranging the Classroom *(cont.)*

Furniture Icons

Use the rectangles or the squares for student desks, depending upon whether your students use group tables or individual desks.

Center	Teacher's Desk		Coat Closet			Classroom Library
Center			Student Desk	Student Desk		Bulletin Board
	Student Table		Student Desk	Student Desk		Bulletin Board
Center			Student Desk	Student Desk		Chalk Board
	Student Table		Student Desk	Student Desk		Chalk Board
Center	Student Table		Student Desk	Student Desk	Student Desk	Student Desk
Center			Student Desk	Student Desk	Student Desk	Student Desk
	Student Table		Student Desk	Student Desk	Student Desk	Student Desk
Center	Student Table		Student Desk	Student Desk	Student Desk	Student Desk
Center			Student Desk	Student Desk	Student Desk	Student Desk
	Student Table		Student Desk	Student Desk	Student Desk	Student Desk
Center	Student Table		Student Desk	Student Desk	Student Desk	Student Desk
Center	Student Table		Display Table			

Arranging the Classroom (cont.)

Here are some important considerations when planning your classroom arrangement:

- **Permanent Fixtures.** Consider where permanent items such as electrical outlets, windows, and bulletin boards are located before arranging your room. Be sure to incorporate them into your classroom map. Teachers have been known to set up their entire classrooms before realizing that the only electrical outlet is inaccessible to the Computer Center or that the Art Center is on the opposite side of the room from the sink.

- **Traffic Flow.** It saves time during rotation and helps maintain order if centers flow logically from one to the other and in the same direction around the room. For example, if you want the Writing Center to follow the Listening Center so that students can respond to a story they heard, the two centers should be adjacent to or near each other. Rotation should be planned to be either clockwise or counterclockwise, so that students do not run into each other as they rotate.

- **Noisy and Quiet Areas.** To reduce the disruption of quiet activities, arrange noisy centers such as the Blocks Center and Puzzles and Games Center together and away from such quiet centers as Reading and Brainstorming.

- **Whole Group Area.** Even though students will be working individually or in small groups, a whole group meeting area is crucial for the entire class to meet for shared reading, class meetings, and whole class instruction. Select a cozy corner or carpeted area that is big enough for everyone to be comfortable but not so big that students lose the feeling of cohesiveness.

- **Storage Space.** A learning center classroom does not need a desk for each student and most likely will not have room for them once centers are set up for active learning. Still, students need space for personal belongings such as jackets, notebooks, and backpacks. Teachers must be creative when it comes to providing personal storage space. Some have used such things as cupboards, laundry baskets, and even large, stacked coffee cans to create individual spaces. You also need storage for manipulatives and supplies. An art center must be filled with supplies to stimulate creativity; a math center must have the objects necessary to learn abstract concepts in a concrete manner. Consider where you will store materials and try to place each center near its requisite manipulatives and supplies.

- **Display Areas.** Provide a display area near its corresponding center. For instance, if you have a bulletin board to display student writing samples, place the Writing Center near it. Students enjoy reading and sharing their stories with others, and it may help students learn to model others' strategies into their own work.

- **Flexibility.** Centers can be against walls, in corners, behind partitions, on tables, on desks, or in storage bins. Consider center needs when arranging your classroom. You may want to make a list of what you have and how it is currently being used. Then you can add alternative possibilities to what you have.

Organizing and Using Centers

Remember that learning something new takes time, patience, and practice. Do not demand or expect perfection when you begin using learning centers. Keep in mind that you will probably change the organization and management of your learning centers several times before arriving at the best format.

Introducing Learning Centers

When making the transition to learning centers, share goals with students and involve them in the evaluation process. Explain why you are starting to use learning centers, and discuss with students the reasons for changes you make. Allow students a role in the development of learning centers. This will affirm the presence and importance of learning centers in the classroom, and it will provide you an opportunity to gain valuable insight into students' feelings about the instructional change.

When beginning to use centers in your classroom, it is important to allow the students time and opportunity to get comfortable with the concept. Initially they may not be at ease, since using centers requires self-motivation and self-confidence. However, as their comfort level rises, so will their confidence and motivation. You may wish to begin with the confidence-building activities on pages 41–43 or the About Me center activities on pages 83–97.

Setting Expectations

Students thrive when the best is expected of them. They will work hard to meet challenges that are within their reach. However, if students are overwhelmed by too many expectations, they can become frustrated, show anxiety, and exhibit behavior problems (Thomas, 1975).* Consequently, it benefits all participants to begin slowly and gradually increase the requirements. For example, the goal for the first week can be to simply understand the schedule and rotation. The activities will be easy, familiar tasks that allow students an opportunity to experience centers and gain an understanding of the approach. The next week, focus may include following directions (reading and rereading, if necessary), increasing the difficulty of the activities, and providing less student assistance. Students need to become independent, responsible individuals. Focusing on the importance of reading directions in the beginning of learning center implementation will assist all students in assuming their roles as active learners.

Learning centers are student-driven. However, they still must be teacher-monitored. In order to do both effectively, you may wish to reproduce the Expectations Contract on page 288 for the centers. Post a contract in each center and have every student who works there to read it and sign it before starting.

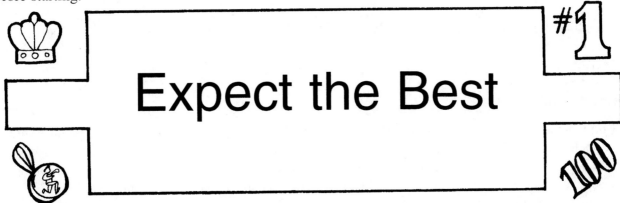

Expect the Best

#1

*Thomas, J.I. *Learning Centers: Opening Up the Classroom.* Holbrook Press 1975.

Organizing and Using Centers *(cont.)*

Positive Reinforcement

Generally, when students feel good about themselves they are more likely to succeed. Crucial to the learning center philosophy is that students take an active part in their education—experimenting and exploring to gain meaningful and relevant knowledge and understanding. In order to do this, students must feel comfortable and safe in the learning environment and be confident that their ventures will be respected and valued. They must know that they will not be criticized, negated, or teased. You must earn your students' trust through positive reinforcement, a behavior management philosophy that focuses on the positive rather than the negative.

Because teachers are responsible for so many students, it is easy to focus on students who are acting inappropriately. Negative behavior tends to receive all the attention, even though it, too, is negative.

> "Jimmy, why haven't you finished your math assignment?"
>
> "Diane, please pay attention."
>
> "If you do not get to work immediately, Tony, I will have to send a note home to your parents."

Conversely, positive reinforcement recognizes the work of students behaving appropriately and attempts to commend them while improving the actions of others. For example, when a student is having difficulty completing his or her work, rather than commenting about the negative behavior, praise another child who is working diligently. Likewise, when students are talking out of turn or disturbing their peers, compliment students who are waiting their turn and being respectful.

> "Carlos, I really like the way you are standing in line so quietly."
>
> "You are doing a super job at the writing station, Kamika."
>
> "I love the way Jamail and Maria are working together on their story."

This positive approach to discipline usually works amazingly well. If a negative behavior persists, simply standing next to or sitting with the disruptive child may work. Any additional intervention should take place privately.

Centers Schedules

Your daily schedule is critical for classroom management. If you or your students are constantly interrupted, behavior problems increase and authentic learning decreases. Determining a schedule that is best for your classroom is a difficult task. Take into consideration the amount of time needed for each subject or set of centers, the availability of instructional assistants or volunteers, lunch and recess breaks, and special-areas and pull-out classes that remove individual students from the classroom.

Organizing and Using Centers *(cont.)*

Starting New Centers

It is important to introduce new centers to the entire class before having students visit them. If students are somewhat familiar with the materials and process, fewer management problems will arise. You may wish to present a lesson such as a science experiment to the whole class and then place all the necessary materials at a center. This allows students to learn the background information necessary to approach their investigation, then gives them more time to explore independently.

Keep in mind that when introducing a new center it is generally not necessary to present a sample or to give the specific directions. It is valuable for students to learn the importance of creative discovery and reading (and rereading) directions. Too often students are told exactly what to do, how to do it, and what it should look like when it's finished. Learning centers provide a safe place for students to think creatively, to solve their own problems, and to be proud of their creativity.

Keys to Success—The 3 C's

Consistency

Learning centers can be a vital, energizing component of a learning program, but in order for the program to be effective students must feel safe and free. Be patient. Consider the first month or two as Centers training time. Make the centers' activities engaging but keep them basic. Allow students adequate time to "learn the ropes" and build their confidence. Once they are secure in the way learning centers work, the benefits of centers will magnify exponentially. Be extremely consistent in the way you manage your centers during this training time.

Clarity

Devise and implement a system that clearly indicates to students when changes occur during Centers time. Nonverbal signals work best, such as different pieces of music, bells, whistles, hand-claps, or on/off flashes of the lights. Students will learn to associate a consistent sound/sight with these periods of Centers time:

- beginning of Centers time
- when to change centers
- two-minute warning and clean-up
- end of Centers time

Color Coding

Color coding is an excellent way to keep your centers organized and your students on task. Be sure to label everything, and do so in vibrant color. Maintain consistency in the color you use for each center, and clearly display the code to guide students. For example, if you color the Math Center sign blue, mark all center materials with blue or duplicate activity pages, expectation contracts, and other information onto blue paper, and provide blue identification tags (clothespins, stickers, etc.) for students who are working in the center. Incorporate consistent color into every possible aspect of using centers, and your reward will be a more smoothly running class and more confident students.

Open Work Time

Open work time provides students a chance to practice the skills they are currently learning as well as those skills that they should have already mastered. If you choose to use centers for open work time, you may wish to consider these suggestions.

Allow students to choose the activity they would like to explore further. Some will choose the same activity for several days if their curiosity is stimulated or if they're becoming expert at the task. This type of practice builds self-esteem. Students tend to choose activities appropriate to their ability level because activities that are too easy or too difficult will not hold their interest. If a child is not able to choose an activity that is appropriate or productive, you may wish to provide guidance.

This block of practice time is quite useful in assessing students. You can hear and see what students are choosing, what they are capable of doing, what they are interested in, and how well they get along with others.

You need to provide many types of activities and provide instructions, modeling, and specific parameters for the use of each. You must also be prepared, willing, and able to explain the skills involved and purposes for each activity to parents and other visitors or volunteers who may be part of this class time.

Remember to provide activities that your class has done previously in formal instruction. Repeating lessons and activities is a very useful learning tool for students. Repetition strengthens the basic lesson for some students while offering improvisation and extension opportunities for others.

Make open work time a fundamental part of the instructional day for each student. Open work time should not be used as a reward for finishing a particular task or for good behavior. Given freedom and encouragement, every student will find at least one activity he or she can perform well and thus experience success.

When students are involved and actively engaged in learning in a supportive, exciting classroom environment, you will see, hear, and feel the excitement and creativity that learning centers can provide. Enjoy!

Getting Comfortable— Grades K-1

This is my name.

_____

- -

_____

| This is me. | This is something I like. |

Getting Comfortable—
Grades 1-3

My name is _____

This is me.

The best thing about me is _____

_____

_____

My favorite thing to do is _____

_____

_____

Getting Comfortable— Grades 4-6

Name_____

If you were to see me, you might say that I _____

_____

_____

_____

_____

_____

If you were to meet me, you would learn that I _____

_____

_____

_____

_____

_____

_____

_____

Some other really important things to know about me are _____

_____

_____

_____

_____

_____

_____

Rotating Students Through Learning Centers

There is a variety of ways to manage the rotation of students through learning centers. Daily rotation provides flexibility in grouping. Weekly rotation allows students to devote more time to each center. Choose the methods that best suit your teaching style, your students, and your classroom. Remember to determine in advance—and post clearly for students to see—the maximum number of students that may work in a center at the same time. The management methods offered in this section of the book may be adapted to any type of Centers system you use:

- Teacher Structured—Students are grouped and directed by teacher to design the centers.

- Individual Choice—The teacher gives students general expectations for Centers time (e.g., read to yourself, write a make-believe story, do a science experiment) and allows students to choose which centers they will use at what time.

- Open Rotation—Students may circulate among the centers at will during free-time exploration.

Centers Chart

Make and use a laminated chart like the one below to show where each student should be working. As students rotate through the centers in assigned groups, change your chart. You may wish to write the permanent words (_____ Center, Red Group, Green Group, perhaps the groups' names) on the chart before you laminate it.

_____ Center	_____ Center
Red Group	**Green Group**
Nicholas	Emily
Alicia	William
Kenneth	May
Travis	Benjamin
Brianna	Robert
Katie	Dottie
_____ Center	_____ Center
Blue Group	**Yellow Group**
Zachary	Linda
Tyler	Barbara
Brittany	Harry
Sean	Nancy
Jessica	Jenna
Brent	Donna

Name Tags

Make a name tag for each student (or let each make his or her own) and have students place their name tags by the center in which they are working. Be sure to limit the number of students allowed in a center at one time. You may wish to reproduce the tags below and laminate them after student's names are on them. If you use color-coded groups, reproduce the cards onto the corresponding colors of paper.

Checkerboard

Following the model shown, students are divided into five groups. Each group completes only one center per day. By the end of the week, every group will have completed each of five centers. Reproduce the blank chart below, and insert your center names and group names or designations. You may wish to color code and/or laminate the chart.

Day	Center #1	Center #2	Center #3	Center #4	Center #5
Monday	A	B	C	D	E
Tuesday	E	A	B	C	D
Wednesday	D	E	A	B	C
Thursday	C	D	E	A	B
Friday	B	C	D	E	A

Day	Center	Center	Center	Center	Center
Monday					
Tuesday					
Wednesday					
Thursday					
Friday					

Centers Cards

Use small cards to record each student's progression through the centers. Each card should have a student's name and the names of all the centers. As the student attends each center, mark the card with a sticker, your initials, or a punched hole. Students must attend each center on the card. A reward (sticker, treasure, applause) can be given each time a student completes his or her card. The student then receives a new card and begins the centers rotation again. A progress sheet can be created by recording the date each student finishes each centers card.

Reproduce, color, and cut out the cards below. Punch a hole where indicated and lace with string or yarn. Let each student wear a card around his or her neck.

Pocket Charts

Create a pocket chart using colorful tagboard and library card pockets. Glue the pockets to the tagboard and laminate. Using a razor blade, cut a slit through the laminate at each pocket opening so the center cards will slide in easily.

With a permanent marker, write a student's name on each pocket. On index cards, draw a picture illustrating the center or write the name of each center. Make as many of each center card as the number of students allowed in that center at one time. (For example, if four students can use the science center at once, make four science cards.) Place the index cards in the pockets.

When you are ready to change centers, move the cards to the right. Be sure to space the cards so that students will not go to the same center two times in a row. (Don't put same-center cards next to each other.) You may wish to reproduce and use one of the record-keeping forms on pages 54–60 so you know when each student has completed each center.

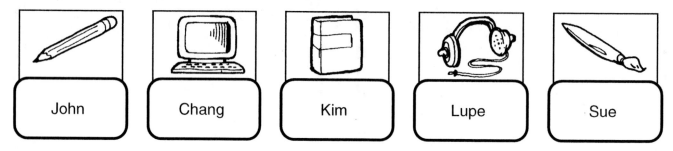

| John | Chang | Kim | Lupe | Sue |

An alternate method is to purchase a pocket chart. In the top row of the pocket chart, place cards naming each group of students. Under each group name, place cards listing the centers. Sequence the centers as in the checkerboard model (page 46) so that only one group is working at a center at a time. When Centers time begins, have students go to the first center listed in their group's column. When that center's time is up, remove the top cards and have students go again to the top card in their column. Do this until you have completed the cycle of centers and the centers pockets are empty.

Red Group	Yellow Group	Green Group	Blue Group
Art	Science	Listening	Math
Math	Art	Science	Listening
Listening	Math	Art	Science
Science	Listening	Math	Art

Clothespins, Craft Sticks, and Cups

The following rotation methods can be adapted for color-coded centers and different student designations (name, number, group). For each rotation method, be sure to keep a record of which centers each student has completed on what date.

Clothespins

Post a tagboard chart listing the centers and the maximum number of students allowed in the center at the same time. Print each student's name on a clothespin. Clip each student's clothespin to the center where he or she is to work. You or your students can move the clothespins to another center when it is time to change centers.

Craft Sticks

Gather library pockets and craft sticks. On each library pocket, write the name of a center and the maximum number of students allowed in the center at the same time. Attach the library pockets to a large piece of tagboard. Write each student's name on a craft stick. At the beginning of Centers time and when it is time to change centers, move the craft sticks into a different center pocket.

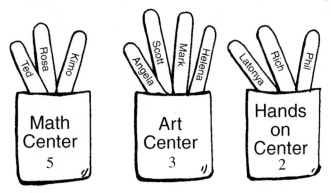

Cups

Divide the class into color-coded groups. Assemble sets of colored cups and sheets of colored stickers that correspond to the groups' colors. During Centers time, have students put one of their colored stickers on the tops of their hands. Place a stack of cups at each center, making sure that the colors are staggered so a group is only designated to be in one center at a time. When Centers time starts, have students go to the center whose top cup matches their stickers. When it is time to change centers, have one student in each group move the top cup to the bottom of the stack. The groups then rotate to the next center based on the color of cup that is now on top.

Rotation Wheels

When using any of these options, be sure to keep a record of which students have completed which centers.

1. Reproduce the pie wheel on page 51, or make your own with the same number of sections as you have centers. Write the name of a center on each section. Attach the wheel to a large chart with the student group designations (color, names, letter, number) around the perimeter. Turn the wheel to indicate which group is to work at which center.

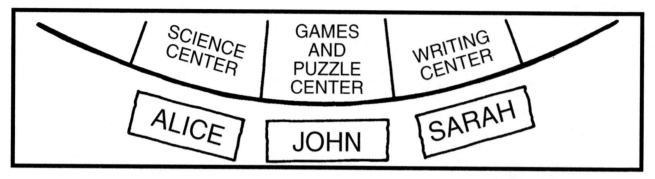

2. Cut two large (but different-sized) circles from construction paper or tagboard. On the outer edge of the larger circle, write the names of the centers. Divide the smaller circle into a corresponding number of sections. Write the names of your students in the sections on the smaller circle. Attach the smaller circle to the larger by punching holes in the centers of both and fastening a brad through it. Turn the circle to indicate which group of children is to work at which center.

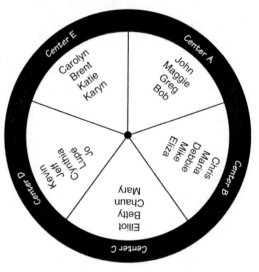

3. Divide the class into four groups (let the groups choose their names) and name four centers. Divide a sheet of tagboard into four equal sections. Make a rotation wheel with only four sections. In each section, write the name of a group. Attach the wheel to the center of the tagboard with a brad. In the tagboard sections outside the wheel, write the names of the four centers. Turn the wheel to indicate which group is to work at which center. You may wish to make more than one wheel chart, depending on the number of centers you have. This system can also be reversed, with the students' names outside the wheel and the centers on the wheel.

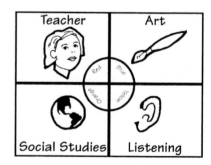

Sample Rotation Wheel

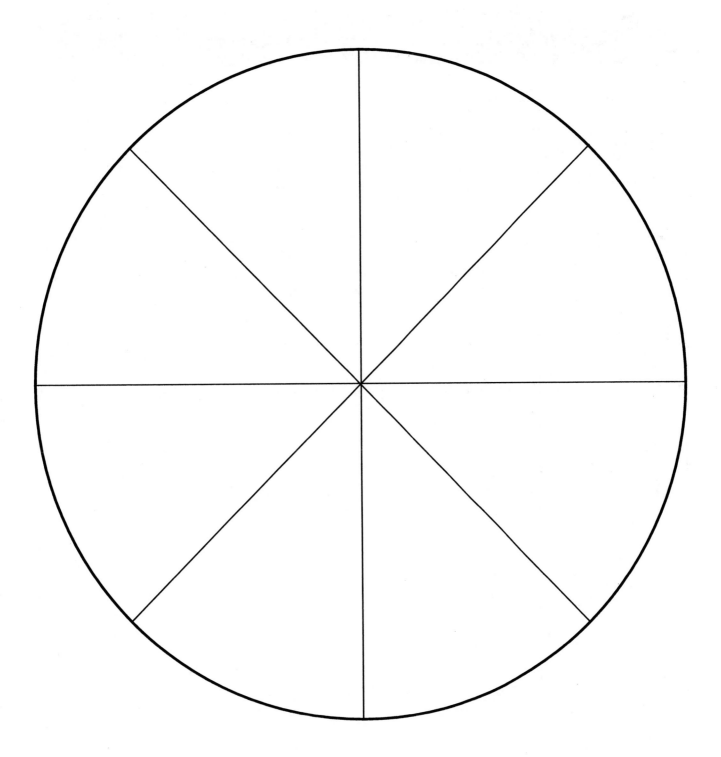

Sample Schedule
Grades 1-3

Time	Schedule
8:45–9:00	Welcome, Attendance, Lunch Count, Flag Salute, Calendar
9:00–10:45	Curriculum Centers (4): Students are placed in four heterogeneous groups for the day and rotate through four centers: Math, Writing, Reading, and Free Choice
10:45–11:00	Theme Centers (8): Students are place in eight groups and complete one center each day. Centers integrate art, writing, problem solving, social studies, reading, computation, spelling, oral language, and cooperative learning.
11:55–12:40	Lunch/Organized Outdoor Games
12:40–1:15	Shared Reading/D.E.A.R. (Drop Everything And Read)
1:15–2:00	Science Lab
2:00–2:45	Monday—Physical Education
	Tuesday—Health
	Wednesday—Music
	Thursday—Library
	Friday—Physical Education

Sample Schedule—Grades 4-6

Time	Schedule
8:15–8:30	Opening, Attendance, Lunch Count, Flag Salute, Sharing
8:30–9:30	Social Studies Centers (two days a week)/Social Studies Whole Group Lesson, Individual Work, or Partner Work (three days a week) (1) Computers/GeoSafari/Social Studies Games (2) Art Activity (3) Writing/Research Assignment (4) Readers Theater—Skit (5) Teacher-Directed Lesson (Review concepts)
9:30–9:45	Mini Grammar Lesson (e.g., common nouns, plural nouns)
9:45–10:30	Writer's Workshop (students placed in six heterogeneous groups) (1) Brainstorming Station (word web) (2) First Draft/Peer Edit Station (3) Teacher Conference Station (4) Second Draft/Cursive Station (5) Publishing Station (Computers)
10:30–10:45	Recess
10:45–11:10	Problem of the Day (Math) & Journal Writing
11:10–11:55	Math Centers (three days a week)/Whole Group Directed Lesson (one day per week)/Independent Work (one day per week) (1) Computers (2) Logic Sheets/Puzzlers (3) Geoboards/Calculators (4) Flash Cards/Multiplication Bingo/Fraction Games/Time/Money (5) Teacher-Directed Group
12:00–12:45	Lunch/Outdoor Games
12:45–1:00	Daily Oral Language
1:00–1:20	Core Literature—Small-group reading from/discussion of literature book
1:20–2:10	Shared Reading/Whole Group Lesson/Readers Workshop (1) *Readers* Theater—skits (2) Poetry (read, rewrite, create) (3) Guided Reading with the Teacher (4) Illustrating Student-Made Books (5) Independent Silent Reading
2:10–2:30	Science Centers (two days per week)/Science Lab (one day per week)/Physical Education (two days per week) (1) Discovery Center (2) Hands-On Activity

Learning Centers Record—A

No matter what management system you choose, it is extremely important that you keep a record of when each student has completed each center on what day. You may wish to reproduce and use one or more of the forms on pages 54–60. They may be used only once and retained for your permanent records or laminated and reused.

Center _____ **Start Date** _____

Monday	Tuesday	Wednesday	Thursday	Friday

Learning Centers Record—B

Center _____

Start Date _____

Monday	Tuesday	Wednesday	Thursday	Friday

Learning Centers Record—C

Completion Date

Start Date

Center

Name

Learning Centers Record—D

Center _____	Start Date _____
Name:	Completion
1.	
2.	
3.	
4.	
5.	
6.	
7.	
8.	
9.	
10.	
11.	
12.	

Learning Centers Record—E

Name: _____ Date: _____

Center	Completion Date	Center	Completion Date
1.		2.	
3.		4.	
5.		6.	
7.		8.	
9.		10.	
11.		12.	

Learning Centers Record—F

Write the name of each center as you work on it. Have the person in charge stamp the marked square when you have completed the center.

Name _____

Start Date _____

Center	Completed	Center	Completed
1		7	
2		8	
3		9	
4		10	
5		11	
6		12	

Learning Centers Record—G

Use this form for young learners.

Name _____ Start Date _____

The center I am working on is . . .   Color the face when you complete the center.

1.	
	😊
2.	😊
3.	😊
4.	😊
5.	😊

Monitoring Choices

There will times when you need to monitor the choices your students are making. For instance, if you allow students to choose which centers to work in, and you notice that a student works at the same center each day or avoids a particular center, you must provide guidance and implement a program that allows choice but also requires participation at all centers.

1. You may wish to use the recording forms on pages 59 or 60. Using either form, you or your students record centers as they are completed. The form may be attached to a folder or packet so that it is easily accessible. You can leave a note or specific directions for any student(e.g., "Jason, please work at Center #4 today and do two of the activities.")

2. Each student can be given a list or wheel of all the centers and activities for the week. Once students complete an activity at a center, they check if off or color it to note that they have completed it.*

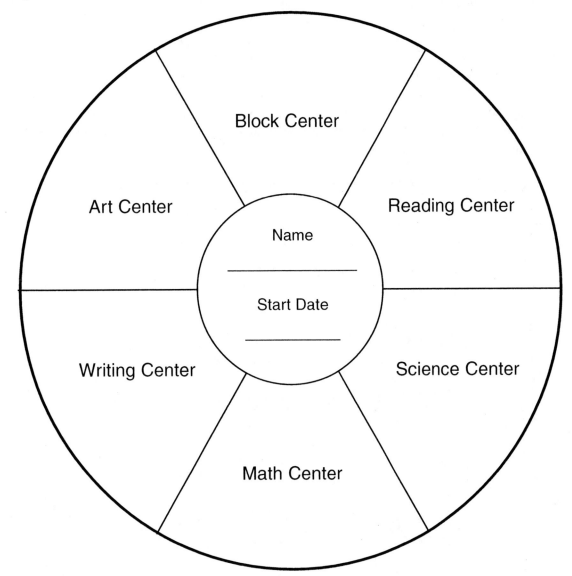

*Pattillo, J., and Vaughan, E. (1992). *Learning centers for child-centered classrooms.* Washington, DC: National Education Association of the United States.

Rules and Guidelines for Learning Centers

Though learning centers provide an atmosphere conducive to independent learning, you must create a balance between freedom and order to offer the best possible learning environment for all your students. To do this, you must establish clear rules, and students must agree to follow them. The best way to ensure that students do that is for them to help make the rules themselves.

Discuss with the class what generally will happen in the learning centers during Centers time, and allow them to tell you what sort of rules and guidelines they think are necessary to make the program successful. As you brainstorm ideas for rules, write them on the chalkboard; then go back through to choose those more specific to learning centers. Once the list is established and the class has agreed, transfer them to a classroom chart or paper form that you can reproduce and post around the classroom and in the centers. A blank form for writing your class set is provided on page 63.

If you prefer to present your class with a set of rules prior to beginning to use learning centers, pages 64–66 provide general sets for kindergarten, Grades 1–3, and Grades 4–6. Feel free to alter them as needed. Give each student a copy of the rules and color and laminate an enlarged copy for display in the classroom. General rules may have to be amended as new situations arise. Review the rules frequently, using a discussion format so that students gain a better understanding of reasons behind each rule. Ask students, "Why should we work cooperatively to solve problems?" Guide them in discovering that cooperation helps all participants by providing multiple ideas and solutions.

Our Learning Centers Rules

Learning Centers Rules for Kindergarten

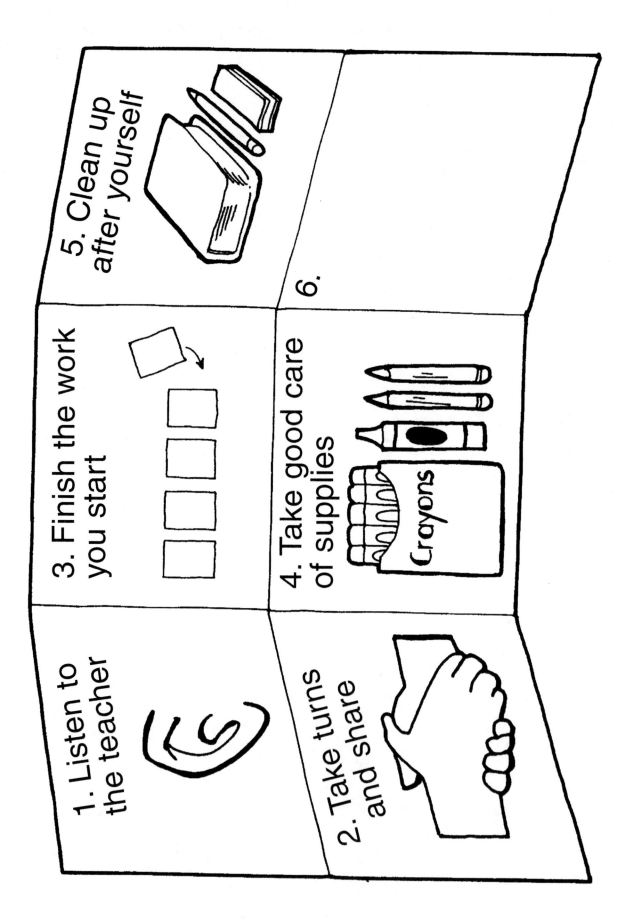

1. Listen to the teacher

2. Take turns and share

3. Finish the work you start

4. Take good care of supplies

Crayons

5. Clean up after yourself

6.

Learning Centers Rules for Grades 1-3

When using the learning centers . . .

1. Be respectful to your teacher and classmates.

2. Do your best.

3. Carefully read and follow all directions.

4. Take care of supplies.

5. Use only one center at a time.

6. Clean up properly before you leave a center.

7. Use indoor voices.

8. _____

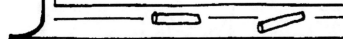

Learning Centers Rules for Grades 4-6

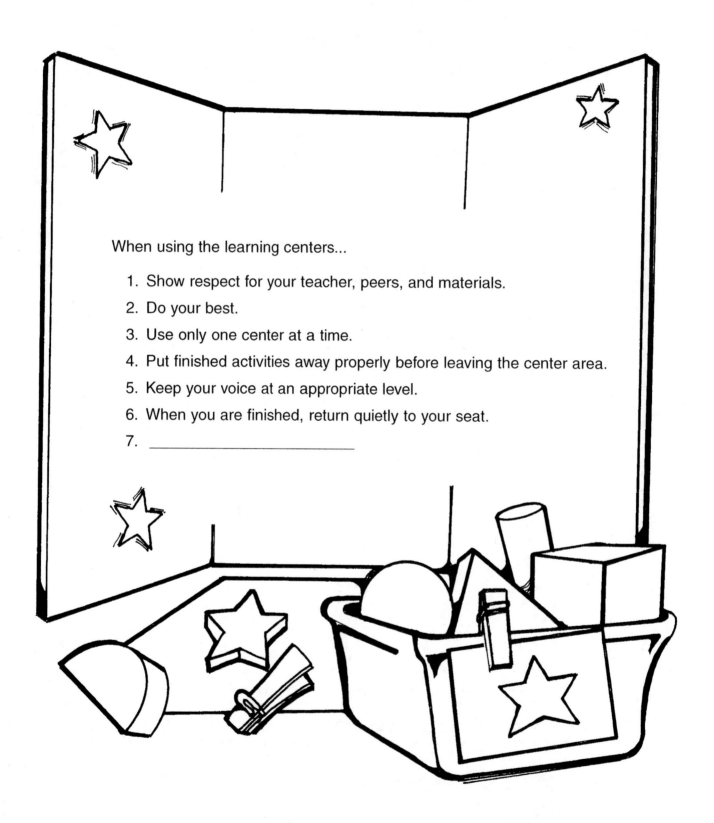

When using the learning centers...

1. Show respect for your teacher, peers, and materials.
2. Do your best.
3. Use only one center at a time.
4. Put finished activities away properly before leaving the center area.
5. Keep your voice at an appropriate level.
6. When you are finished, return quietly to your seat.
7. _____

Storage

Learning centers facilitate a sense of community; individuals become part of a whole, taking responsibility for each other and their environment. The process of establishing a system to manage materials and supplies can be complex as well as time consuming; however, once the learning centers classroom is organized, maintenance is simple, as students know where materials belong and assume responsibility for cleaning up after they are finished with center activities.

You may wish to list all of the materials needed for each center on the directions. Students can plan ahead by reading what they need and making sure each item is available. This also helps during cleanup.

Shelves, supply carts, boxes, and manila envelopes can all be used to store center materials. The art center, for instance, may have a supply cart with creative materials. The reading corner can be made of bookshelves, color-coded baskets for book levels, and cardboard boxes covered in contact paper. Boxes can also be used to hold student work folders and files. Manila envelopes can be laminated to hold small games or puzzles. Attaching a title and direction card to the envelope before laminating is beneficial.

For student supplies, you may wish students to bring shoe boxes from home to store pencils, crayons, and other items. This way, when students move from one center to another, they simply take their boxes with them.*

Regardless of the materials used and the storage space available, it is imperative that items be clearly labeled, accessible to students, and presented in an organized fashion. That is, math materials should be located together and not dispersed throughout the room. Likewise, students in the Listening Center should not have to travel a great distance or search the room for story tapes. Planning ahead and organizing materials can make an enormous difference in classroom management. When items students need are carefully organized, disruptions are kept to a minimum.

*Poppe, C.A., & Van Matre, N.A. (1985). *Science Learning Centers for the Primary Grades*. West Nyack, NY: The Center for Applied Research in Education, Inc.

Pails and Canisters

Inexpensive paint pails, aluminum canisters, and beach buckets make wonderful storage containers for learning center materials. They are sturdy, easy to decorate and label, and completely portable. Even the youngest students can move them around with ease.

Determine how many centers you will have and provide a receptacle for each. Label the receptacles and the materials you place inside them. If possible, color code everything so its correct storage place can be determined at a glance.

You may wish to reproduce the label below and use it to identify your containers.

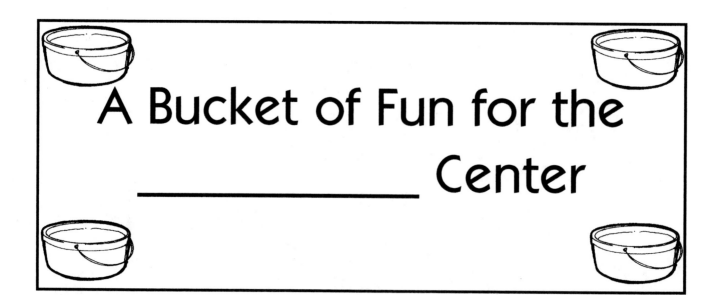

Carts, Boxes, and Crates

Storage carts are wonderfully portable, spacious, and sturdy. Use them to store all supplies for one center or to store supplies common to all centers. They can be wheeled around the room at everyone's convenience. Tiers can be labeled accordingly. You may wish to reproduce and use the label below.

Flat cardboard storage boxes can be purchased from many places. They are relatively inexpensive and are made to fit under a standard bed. Use them to store and stack materials for your various centers. They are ideal if you have large supplies or a variety of things that need to be stored flat. They are easily stacked and can be housed on closet shelves, above cupboards, or even against a wall. Be sure to label your boxes.

Plastic crates, readily available at large hardware stores, provide simple solutions to storage troubles. They, too, stack easily. Depending on the materials you store in them, you may wish to line them with cardboard or even plastic trash can liners.

Everything You Need for

_____

Student Supply Boxes

You may choose to have students carry supplies with them to each center. Here are two ways to make colorful, personal storage boxes.

Materials:

- 1 shoe box per student
- 2 name labels per student
- wrapping paper
- scissors
- tape
- crayons or markers

Directions:

1. Have students use wrapping paper to separately cover the box and lid of their shoe box. (If your students are very young, you may wish to have them wrap their boxes at home with an adult's help.)

2. Have students color their labels, write their names on them, and attach them to the short ends of their boxes.

3. Provide a place for the boxes, and have students stack them with a labeled end facing out.

Materials:

- 1 shoe box per student
- 2 name labels per student
- construction paper
- scissors
- glue
- wide clear tape or clear contact paper
- crayons or markers

Directions:

1. Have students cut shapes and designs from construction paper and glue them onto their boxes and lid, entirely covering any print that might be on the box.

2. When the boxes are decorated, have students "laminate" the entire boxes and lids (separately) with strips of tape or pieces of contact paper.

3. Have students color their labels, write their names on them, and attach them to the short ends of their boxes.

4. Provide a place for the boxes, and have students stack them with a labeled end facing out.

Student Folders or Notebooks

Students need some way to store their work papers until they have been checked and they may take them home. Pocket folders and three-ring notebooks work well. Or you may wish to provide file folders for students to store their papers in. Have students decorate and label their folder, then laminate them for durability. For larger folders, follow these directions:

Materials:

- 2 file folders per student
- clear tape
- laminating machine
- scissors
- crayons or markers
- razor blade (for teacher's use only

Directions:

1. Place a pair of folders side-by-side, overlapping them slightly.

2. Tape both sides of the overlapping seam with clear tape.

3. Have students decorate and label their folders.

4. Help students laminate the large folders, as shown below. Leave about ¹/₃" (.75 cm) on the left and right edges to seal the folders' ends.

5. Be sure the folders can open and close. You may need to slice the top and bottom edges of the laminate for this.

6. Store the folders in a large cardboard storage box.

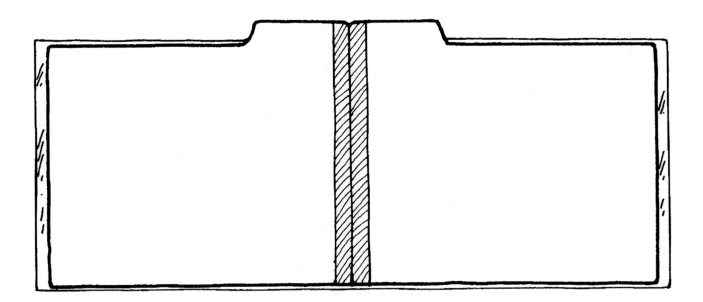

Choosing Materials

The more opportunities students have to interact with materials in different ways (sight, touch, sound, etc.) the more meaningful their learning will be. Ideal materials allow students to learn directly from personal and individual manipulation with little or no adult supervision or intervention. Through manipulation and freedom to explore, children become active rather than passive learners.

Play is an integral part of the learning process, particularly for younger students, but all students benefit greatly from being allowed to make discoveries with concrete objects. For example, nesting blocks teach students how to put things in a series through discovery. If the blocks are placed in a center, students will stack them—often with no instruction at all. When it is time to clean up, students will naturally return the blocks to their original nesting positions. Adults can interact with students to help them add to their language skills by using new words and concepts, such as small–smaller–smallest, large–larger–largest, size, and in order.

If you want to create a written record of what students have learned, have students order and trace the blocks in different ways on a large piece of paper and label them.

Provide extension learning by putting related materials in other centers. For example, place rods of different lengths and blocks that make number stairs in the Math Center or put measuring cups in the Science Center. Have three different-sized stuffed bears with three different-sized bowls in the Drama Center. Books that emphasize differences in size, such as *Goldilocks and the Three Bears* and *The Three Billy Goats Gruff*, may be placed both in the Drama Center and the Library Center.

Keep in mind that the more materials available to students, the greater the chance they will find something they are successful at and therefore become more engaged in active learning.

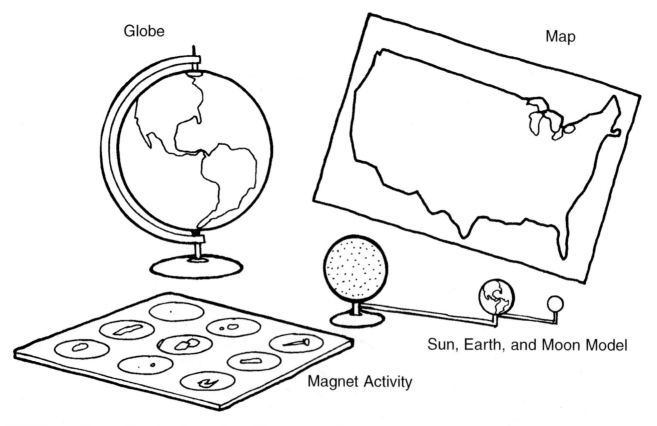

Globe

Map

Sun, Earth, and Moon Model

Magnet Activity

Materials List

Many standard items should be readily available for students to use during Centers time. Add to this list as you prepare activities for each center to create a comprehensive list of materials you will need each year.

You will want to always have on hand such basic materials as writing paper, construction paper, pencils, crayons, markers, glue, scissors, rulers, paint, brushes, and chalk.

You may wish to reproduce the Request for Supplies letter on page 74 to send home with students to help you accumulate many of the things you will need.

Basic materials may be housed at each center, or students can use a box to carry personal supplies from center to center. If materials cannot be stored directly at each center, place them in a central location that is accessible to all centers.

- ❏ plastic straws
- ❏ salt and pepper in shakers
- ❏ dishwashing detergent
- ❏ cooking oil
- ❏ toothpicks
- ❏ white vinegar
- ❏ plastic and paper cups in a variety of colors and sizes
- ❏ butcher twine or string
- ❏ safety goggles
- ❏ masking tape
- ❏ blocks of varying sizes and shapes
- ❏ flashlight and batteries
- ❏ magnets
- ❏ magnifying glasses
- ❏ modeling clay
- ❏ bowls
- ❏ funnel
- ❏ metal teaspoon (5 mL)
- ❏ stopwatch or clock with a second hand
- ❏ bucket (if a sink is not available)
- ❏ rubber bands

- ❏ paper clips
- ❏ scrap paper
- ❏ paper towels
- ❏ soda bottles
- ❏ egg cartons
- ❏ buttons, bottle caps, beans
- ❏ plastic bags
- ❏ baby food jars
- ❏ frozen juice/soup cans
- ❏ margarine tubs and lids
- ❏ fabric scraps
- ❏ old game pieces
- ❏ brown lunch bags
- ❏ sponges
- ❏ cardboard and shoe boxes
- ❏ dress-up clothes and jewelry
- ❏ kitchen/store supplies
- ❏ books, magazines, and newspapers
- ❏ tape recorder, head sets, blank tapes
- ❏ calculators
- ❏ play money
- ❏ computers and software

Request for Supplies

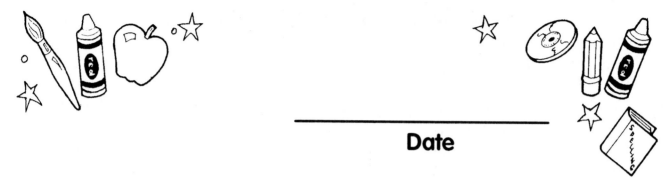

_____
Date

Dear Parent,

Our classroom is organized into diverse and engaging learning centers so that your child can work and learn at his or her own pace and in his or her own way. Many of our activities use items you may have at home. Please take a few moments to see if you have any of the following items on hand.

_____

_____

_____

_____

If you do and would like to help out our class with a contribution, please send the item(s) to school with your child.

Thank you!

_____
Teacher

Supplies Checklist for Kindergarten–Grade 1

Reproduce and cut out the following list for each center. Circle the items that are needed and add any that are missing. Display the list for students to see.

Welcome to the _____ Center.

You will need:

paper

paint

scissors

colored paper

crayons or markers

tape

paste or glue

pen

pencil

computer

Supplies Checklist for Grades 2-6

Reproduce and cut out the following list for each center. Fill in the list of items that are needed and display it for students to see.

Welcome to the _____ Center.

You will need the following supplies:

_____

_____

_____

_____

_____

_____

_____

_____

_____

_____

_____

_____

_____

Be sure to check for supplies before you begin. Also, be sure to leave the supplies in the center when you are finished.

Kindergarten Centers

Kindergarten centers are unique unto themselves. Be sure to model the behaviors you want students to follow in each center.

Take-Apart Center

Materials: empty shoe boxes; rubber mallets; screwdrivers; pliers; measuring tapes; handyman aprons with pockets; old appliances such as toasters, can openers, hair dryers, radios, and clocks **(Note: Cut off all electrical plugs!)**

Directions: Have students take apart items and place pieces into a shoe box for transfer to the Fix-It Center.

Fix-It Center

Materials: handyman aprons; glue; tape (electrical or masking); scissors; screwdrivers; small screws; needlepoint (dull-tipped) needles and heavy-duty thread; buttons; measuring tape; items to be fixed such as the take-apart items; clothing with rips or missing buttons; broken toys; torn pictures

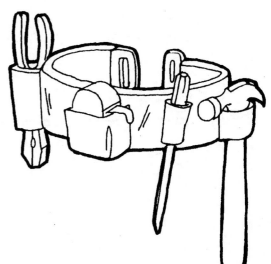

Directions: Have students repair the broken items at the center.

Invention Center

Materials: various sizes and shapes of empty boxes and cans; egg cartons; plastic soda bottles; foam meat trays; plastic vegetable baskets; string; yarn; cloth; felt; colored paper; tissue paper; sequins; buttons; fake fur; aluminum foil; scissors; rulers; paste or glue; crayons; paint; etc.

Directions: Have students invent and build robots, creatures, and devices. **(Note:** When introducing this center, read about or explain what an inventor does. Show pictures of inventions.) Have students share their new inventions with the class.

Read the Walls Center

Materials: old pairs of glasses (with lenses removed); funny play glasses; pointers such as a traditional wooden or metal pointer, pencils with holiday toppers, magic wands, feathers, plastic sword, etc.; and a large box to store items

Directions: Divide students into pairs. Have one student choose a pointer and role play the teacher; the other chooses a pair of glasses and is the reader. The two students move freely around the room, the "teacher" pointing to and the "reader" reading any visible text on the walls. Students may also choose to read student-created enrichment books, books from the class library, or any other items containing text. Students switch roles. **(Note:** Younger students may not read the exact text or point to the exact words as they are "reading." Don't worry about it—this activity will develop naturally as students gain more language and reading experience.)

Kindergarten Centers *(cont.)*

Each grading period, choose one letter. All activities in the center will start with or incorporate the chosen letter. Below are examples of two chosen letters and corresponding activities.

"N" Center

1. Names: Play a variation of hangman using a pocket chart, alphabet-lettered index cards (you'll need multiples of common letters), and a class roster. To play: Allow one student (chooser) to pick a name that he or she wants the other players to try to guess. Then have the chooser pick the letter index cards to spell the name and place them in pocket spaces with the letters facing back. The players count to see how many letters are in the name and take turns guessing letters. If a guessed letter is in the name, the chooser turns over that card. If the letter is not in the name, the chooser writes the letter on scratch paper or dry-erase board. When the name is guessed, all cards are turned around and each player says something nice about that student.

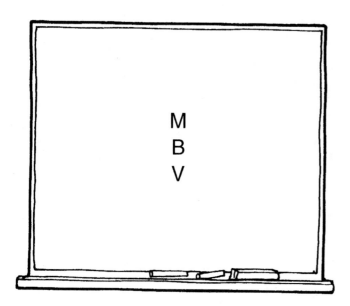 

2. Nursery: Provide a rocking chair, doll furniture, dolls, diapers, baby clothes, feeding utensils and other items usually found in a child's nursery. Allow students to role play caring parents. Provide a variety of books for students to read to their "children."

3. Night Sky: Provide books and activities for students to understand and appreciate the stars in the night sky.

Kindergarten Centers *(cont.)*

"N" Center *(cont.)*

4. Noodles: Provide various sizes and shapes of colored pasta. (To dye pasta, place one cup of white vinegar and ten drops of food coloring in a bowl and stir. Add two to three cups of uncooked pasta; mix until evenly colored. Remove with slotted spoon and dry on wax paper or cookie sheet overnight. Store in self-sealing plastic bags or containers.) Have students use the pasta to create patterns, as math manipulatives, to spell words and form numbers, to create pictures, and to make jewelry.

5. Neighbors: Provide activities and books about community helpers and being a good neighbor. Encourage students to work together to role play cleaning the neighborhood park, having a block party, or being a community helper. If possible, have students watch a video of "Mister Roger's Neighborhood."

"T" Center

1. Textures: Provide a variety of textured items. Allow students to classify the items by placing them in boxes or on cards labeled with texture words. Have students spell words, numbers, or letters by tracing with their fingers on top of sandpaper, in a box filled with salt or rice, or by gluing textured shapes to a pattern. Provide free exploration experiences by allowing students to create a textured project. Place books with touch-and-feel pages in the center area so students can feel the pages as well as read them.

2. Transparencies: Place a piece of white butcher paper on the wall (near ground level) to act as a screen. On the floor, position an overhead projector a few feet away from the paper screen. Provide clear plastic sheets, dry-erase markers, and cloth erasers. Students work together to write spelling words, figure out math problems, and create stories on the overhead using the plastic sheets and markers. Students edit and evaluate their work by reading what's on the butcher paper screen. Remind students that when they are finished they need to snap the marker caps on tightly and erase the plastic sheets

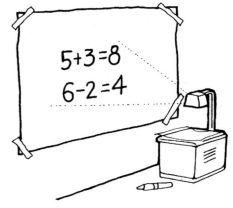

3. Teeth: Provide models of teeth, toothbrushes, pictures of teeth (all available through local dentists or school nurses), and books about teeth, visiting the dentist, and eating healthy foods. If possible, provide a white coat and chair for students to role play visiting the dentist.

4. Television: Using a cardboard box, make a TV set that will fit over students' heads. When a group of students goes to this center, one student will become the TV Teacher by placing the box TV over his or her head. The TV Teacher chooses what to teach the other students at the center. He or she may read a story, ask questions, give a pop quiz, or let the students ask the TV Teacher questions. Have the TV Teacher set a timer for four or five minutes to signal when to "switch channels" and let someone else have a turn.

Kindergarten Centers *(cont.)*

Creative Play Time

Always keep plenty of paper and writing utensils available at your Creative Play Centers to encourage creative writing and artistic expression. Know that when children are engaged in Creative Play Centers time they often choose to incorporate components of two or more centers. For example, students may cooperatively decide they want to create a dramatic play about moms and dads. They start at the Imagination Station Center to get "dressed up," move to the Family Center to pick up their "baby," and go to the Theater Center to perform their impromptu play. This is appropriate and should be encouraged. The only expectation placed on students who move among the centers is that when it is time to clean up, they will put their "borrowed" items back in the correct centers so they will be in their proper places.

Management Using Know–Go–Show

Creative play implies unrestricted freedom to choose activities. To add the component of promoting individual thinking strategy experiences, you may wish to incorporate the Know–Go–Show method. Students still have the freedom to explore creatively, but they also become accountable/responsible for their chosen actions. After children utilize the three-step process for a while they become more reflective about making choices, considering changes, and realizing consequences.

Know (5 minutes)

Have students write their names and the day's date on individual Creative Play forms (page 81) and decide which centers they think they will go to during the Go time period. To show their plan of action, they simply mark appropriate spaces on the forms and place them in a personal cubby or folder.

Go (30 minutes)

This is the actual creative play time. Adult supervision is kept to a minimum. This is essential so children develop higher level critical thinking skills. They need to become responsible for such things as determining when too many are in a center area, how to cooperate in sharing items, and keeping mental track of what they did during the creative play period. Signal a five-minute cleanup period at the end of the Go period.

Show (20 minutes)

Allow students about ten minutes to complete their Creative Play forms by indicating where they went during Go period and drawing pictures about their creative play time. Use the remaining time to let students share their day's activities with others in a whole group context, in small groups, or with partners. You may wish to offer general suggestions or comments about the day's creative play period. If you anticipate changing a center or activity, explain this to students so they have time to think about trying the new center or activity during the next creative play time.

Creative Play Form

Name _____ Date _____

I know I want to:

So I will **go** to:

Now I will **show** you what I did:

About Me

This section provides activities that are very useful in getting students initially involved in learning centers. The About Me Center allows students to focus on themselves.

My Unique Family

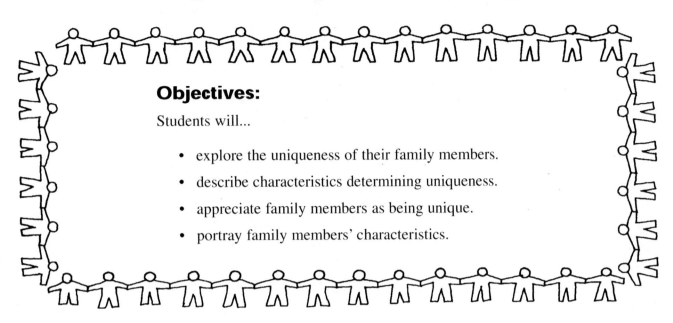

Objectives:

Students will...

- explore the uniqueness of their family members.
- describe characteristics determining uniqueness.
- appreciate family members as being unique.
- portray family members' characteristics.

Materials:

- construction paper "face" circles (in various skin tones)
- crayons and markers (including skin-toned)
- yarn (hair colored, cut into 6-inch /15 cm pieces)
- white glue
- scissors
- assorted paper and fabric scraps, buttons, beans, rice, etc.

Directions:

1. Reproduce several face circles (page 84) for each student. Use a variety of skin-toned paper, if possible.

2. Have students use the circles and materials to create the faces of their family members. Encourage your students to recognize and show the physical similarities and differences among their family members.

3. Have students think about other ways their family members are similar and different, e.g., likes and dislikes, personality traits, etc. Have them write these traits on the backs of the "faces."

Extensions:

Have students create family albums by gluing their family portraits onto construction paper pages. Family albums can be supplemented by adding actual photographs of family members.

Student Direction Card:

Using the provided materials, create each member of your family. On the back of the portraits write things about each person that make him or her unique.

My Unique Family *(cont.)*

Cut out the circle. Color and decorate to make a family member.

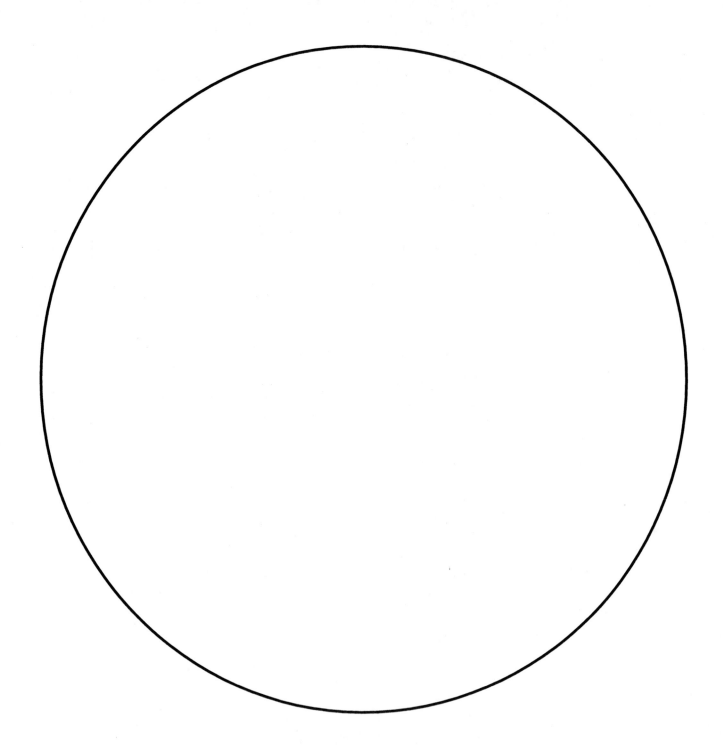

A Book About Me

Objectives:

Students will...

- explore information related to the self.
- share information related to the self.
- describe themselves through drawings.
- learn more about themselves through measurement.
- recognize themselves as important.

Materials:

- construction paper for covers
- About Me book pages
- paper clips, erasers, measuring tapes, and playing cards for measuring
- pencils and crayons or markers

Directions:

1. Make a sample book about yourself to model for students what to do. Discuss each page as you share your book with the class. Students will love to hear all about you and you will have an opportunity to show your work expectations, such as using color and detail in the drawings, correct spelling, and neat handwriting.

2. Reproduce pages 86–93 for each student and explain to students how to complete them. Allow students to ask questions and express concerns about each page.

3. Give each student a packet of book pages, and remind students to incorporate detail into their drawings. Emphasize using correct and careful spelling.

Teacher Tips:

1. You may wish to provide a copy of the book *Me on the Map* by Joan Sweeney (Crown Publishers, 1996) for students to use to complete page 91.

2. Also provide several maps for modeling and a clear example of a map key.

Extension:

Display the About Me books in the classroom for several days before sending them home, so that students can read about their classmates. Information pages that reinforce your curriculum can be added to the books, such as a map of the student's neighborhood, an hourly chart of daily activities, or a written interview with someone in the student's family.

Student Direction Card:

Using the pages provided, create an About Me book. Use color and detail in your work. Be sure to write and spell carefully.

A Book About Me *(cont.)*

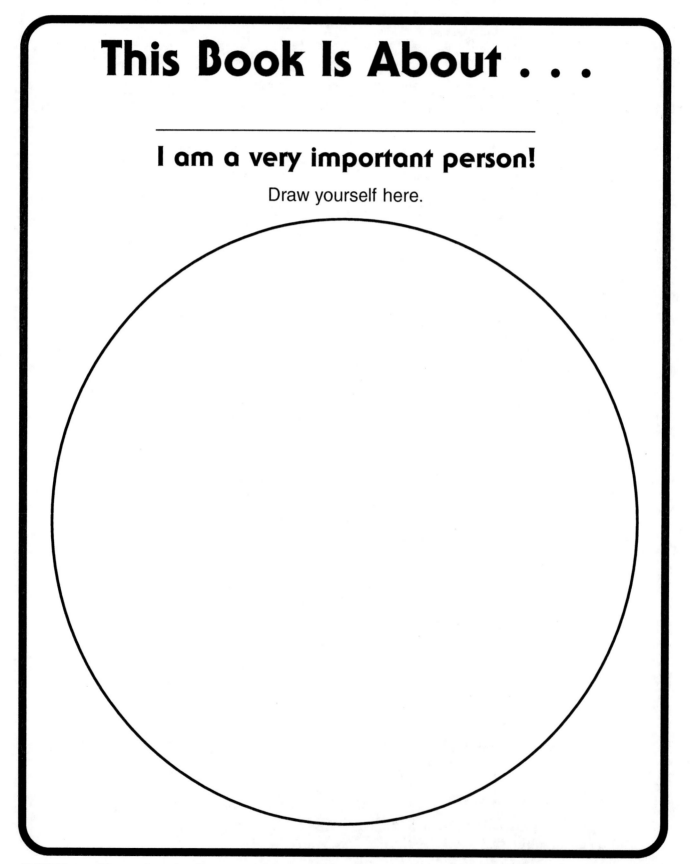

This Book Is About . . .

_____

I am a very important person!

Draw yourself here.

A Book About Me (cont.)

My Favorite Things

Draw or list your favorite things.

Colors	**Foods**
Animals	**Books**
Hobbies	**Places**
People	**Subjects**

A Book About Me *(cont.)*

About My School

Fill in the blanks.

My school is called _____.

I am in the _____ grade.

My teacher's name is _____.

I am in room _____.

I get to school by _____.

School starts at _____.

The rules we follow are:

_____

_____

_____

_____

_____

_____

_____

_____

_____

_____

_____

_____

A Book About Me *(cont.)*

How I Measure Up

Fill in the blanks.

1. My name, _____, has _____ letters.

2. I am _____ rulers tall.

3. My head is _____ playing cards around.

4. My hand is _____ erasers long.

5. My arm is _____ hands long.

6. My elbow is _____ inches around.

7. My shoe is _____ centimeters long.

8. My knee is _____ crayons from my ankle.

9. My wrist is _____ erasers from my elbow.

10. My thumb tip is _____ centimeters from my pinkie tip.

11. My leg is _____ inches long.

12. My hair is _____ paper clips long.

A Book About Me *(cont.)*

My Memories

Draw or write responses to each of the prompts.

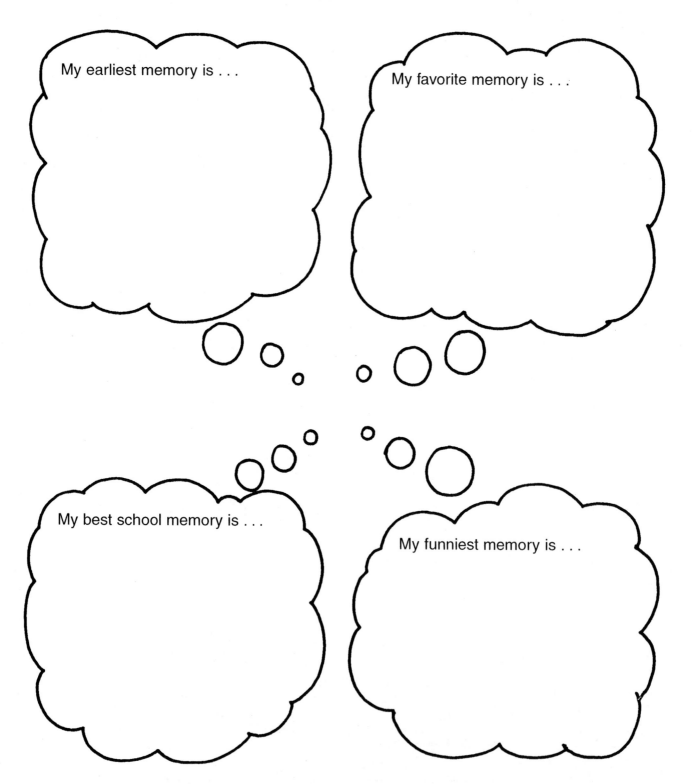

A Book About Me *(cont.)*

Me on the Map

Draw a map of your home in the space below. Draw yourself in your favorite spot. Add at least ten important or special features of your home. Draw a map key to identify the features.

Key

A Book About Me *(cont.)*

My Dream for the Future

Draw and write about your dream for the future.

Key

A Book About Me (cont.)

My Word!

Trace your hand in the space below. Inside your hand, write ten or more words that describe you. Some words you might include are: kind, happy, helpful, athletic, smart, joyful, sincere, polite, generous, loving, brave, honest, caring, funny, nice. Cut out your hand and the border and glue it to the inside of your About Me book cover.

Picture Puzzles

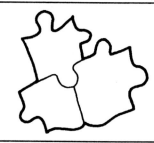

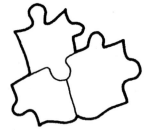

Objectives:

Students will...

- describe themselves through drawings.
- create puzzles.

Materials:

- drawing and construction paper
- large envelopes
- crayons or markers
- glue sticks
- scissors
- full-length mirror (optional)

Directions:

1. Have students draw, on large drawing paper, a picture of their whole bodies. Encourage students to pay attention to proportional details. You may want to provide a full-length mirror for students to study themselves.

2. Provide students with glue sticks and have them cover the entire back of their drawings and mount them on construction paper.

3. Show students how to draw cutting lines on the back of the construction paper to create eight sections about the same size but in different shapes. (The shapes of the pieces should vary.)

4. Have students cut along the lines to create a puzzle.

5. Give each student a large envelope and have him or her decorate and label it. Have students put their picture puzzles in their envelopes.

6. Leave the envelopes in the center so other students can have fun putting the puzzles together.

Extensions:

1. Give each student a number with which to label their envelopes instead of with his or her name. This will allow other students to guess who is in the puzzle pictures. A chart can be made from a class list to record the students' guesses. Have students try to match the code numbers to their classmates' names. Identities can be revealed once everyone has had a chance to guess.

2. Use the puzzles for a class puzzle party. Give each student a puzzle to put together and have him or her try to guess who created it. You may wish to award prizes for correct guesses.

Student Direction Card:

Use the drawing paper to draw a picture of yourself, including as much detail as possible. Then glue your drawing to a piece of construction paper. Next, draw light cutting lines on the back of the construction paper. Make eight sections that are about the same size but of different shapes. Cut on the lines to create your puzzle. Store your puzzle in a large envelope.

This Is Me

Objectives:

Students will...

- describe themselves by making personalized collages.
- share aspects of themselves.

Materials:

- person pattern
- tagboard or cardboard
- large paper
- magazines
- scissors
- pencils
- glue

Directions:

1. Enlarge the pattern on page 96, draw around it onto tagboard, and cut it out with an art knife to create a sturdy pattern.
2. Have students trace the pattern onto large pieces of paper and cut them out. Have students write their names on one side.
3. Allow students time to find and cut out magazine pictures that show something about themselves. Encourage students to cut pictures out carefully, removing any unnecessary writing.
4. Brainstorm with students the kinds of things they may find: pictures that show things they like to do or eat, hobbies, collections, pets, personality traits, etc.
5. Have students glue their pictures on their people cut-outs.
6. Display the collages in the classroom and have students guess who the outlines represent.

Teacher Tips:

1. Create a collage of yourself to model for students. Laminate it so you can use it for several years.
2. Be sure your tagboard outline is a reasonable size. Too large of an area to cover with pictures can discourage students. Too small of an area can limit their creativity.

Extensions:

Place the collages on the hallway walls outside your classroom, or use them during open house or parent night events.

Student Direction Card:

Trace the person pattern onto a large piece of paper. Write your name on one side of your traced person. Find pictures in magazines that show things about yourself—likes, hobbies, personality traits, favorite colors, food, movies, etc. Cut out magazine pictures and glue them onto the blank side of your person.

Person Pattern

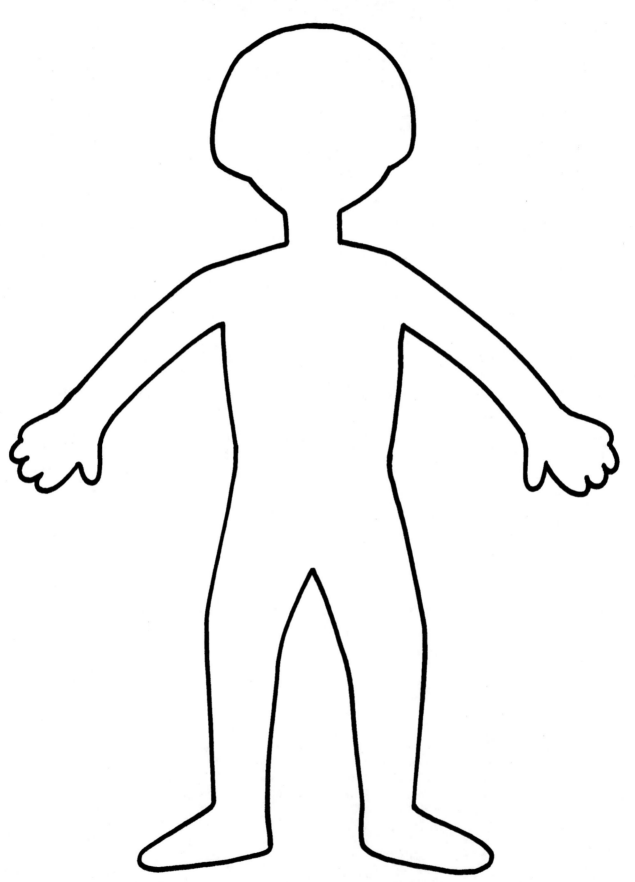

My Family Tree

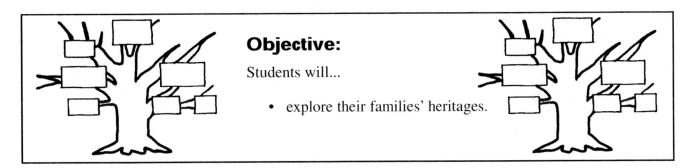

Objective:

Students will...

* explore their families' heritages.

Materials:

* large drawing paper
* finger paint
* large, flat containers for paint
* markers

Directions:

1. Draw several trees on the chalkboard. Ask your students to help with design ideas. Point out the common features of the trees, as well as their unique elements.
2. Tell students to include roots, trunks, and branches when they create their own tree drawings. Remind students that their drawings will have some common features but each will still be unique.
3. After students have drawn their trees, have them use finger paint to put handprint "leaves" on the trees. Tell them to put one "leaf" for each member of their family, including themselves.
4. When the paint is dry, have students label each leaf with a family member's name.
5. Lead the class in a discussion of family heritages as students show their trees to the class.
6. Guide students to recognize the differences between the trees. Stress that all trees (families), no matter how many leaves, have some things in common. Discuss these common factors with your students, suggesting such things as love, caring, and the freedom to be yourself. Be sensitive to the individual issues and needs of your students.

Teacher Tips:

1. Discuss family diversity and point out that many living situations constitute a family.
2. Provide scrap paper for students to practice making handprints before putting them on their trees.

Extensions:

1. Create a class graph to show the different family situations in your classroom.
2. Bring in a tree branch and attach pictures of the students to it. Encourage the students to consider their classmates as their "school family."

Student Direction Card:

Draw a large tree. Use finger paints to create handprint leaves on your tree. Make one leaf for each member of your family. When the paint is dry, label each leaf with a family member's name. Be sure to include yourself.

Skills Development

One of the goals of education is to develop independent learners. Students must become proficient in using study skills in order to obtain and process information on their own. Most study skills are included under the following general headings:

1. Locating information
2. Making judgments about the material
3. Organizing and summarizing
4. Identifying and remembering important information
5. Developing good study habits

Each of these headings can be further subdivided into specific skills such as using a table of contents, deciding whether the material is fact or opinion, taking notes, using mnemonic devices as memory aids, or having a consistent time and place to study.

As soon as students start academic learning, teachers need to start teaching study skills, and this valuable learning tool must be reinforced by all teachers throughout a student's school years.

All students, whether they practice and study in groups or alone, need techniques to help make the most of their studying time. Using learning centers allows teachers to introduce and reinforce study skills throughout the school year. Centers activities do not have to be limited to areas of the curriculum. A learning skills center that teaches students how they can learn better is a valuable addition to your center activities. Here are some performance tasks and their descriptions that may help in planning your skill-based centers.

Comparison Task: The student is required to compare two or more people, places, or things.

Classification Task: The student is asked to classify, or put into categories, certain people, places, or things.

Position Support Task: The student is asked to take a position on a subject or issue and defend that position.

Application Task: The student is asked to apply his or her knowledge in a new situation.

Analyzing Perspectives Task: The student is asked to analyze two or three different perspectives and then choose the perspective he or she supports.

Decision Making Task: The student must identify the factors that caused a certain decision to be made.

Historical Perspective Task: The student must consider differing theories to answer basic historical questions.

Prediction Task: The student must make predictions about what could have happened or will happen in the future.

Problem Solving Task: The student must create a solution to a specific problem.

Experiment Task: The student sets up an experiment to test a hypothesis.

Invention Task: The student must create something new and unique.

Error Identification Task: The student must identify specific errors.

Skills Development (cont.)

It is important in skills development centers to create activities that students can use to practice specific skills. For example, although the main emphasis in teaching reading has shifted away from acquiring isolated skills, students still need some practice in areas like alphabet recognition, phonics, and reading comprehension.

Students now learn skills in relation to the literature they are studying. To support this type of learning, you can create manipulatives and games that foster learning. These can be packaged in small see-through containers and/or plastic bags and placed in a Skills Center or the Reading Center. Each packet serves one or two students. Often children work in pairs since it encourages vocabulary development and verbalization of learning strategies.

Matching Center Materials to Test Objectives

1. Objective: Use antonyms as clues to the meanings of new words.

   Skill Packet: Provide opposites cards for matching.

2. Objective: Arrange events in sequential order.

   Skill Packet: Sequence scrambled picture cards or sentences.

3. Objective: Describe the setting of a story.

   Skill Packet: Furnish writing materials and pictures of places from magazines or small study prints. Students choose a picture and write a short description. Staple the picture to the student's work.

4. Objective: Identify cause-and-effect relationships.

   Skill Packet: Supply cause-and-effect cards for matching and/or describing in writing.

5. Objective: Understand the feelings and emotions of characters.

   Skill Packet: Match drawings of facial emotions to drawings of related situations.

Tip: Look at the literature you are reading to get ideas for pictures that show emotions. Match a picture of a birthday cake and presents to a picture of a child's happy face after reading *Mop Top* by Don Freeman (Viking, 1955). Match a scared face to an alligator under a bed after reading *There's an Alligator Under My Bed* by Mercer Mayer (Dial, 1987). You may wish to have older students match a sentence with each face.

6. Objective: Distinguish between fact and opinion.

   Skill Packet: Sort real and make-believe cards. Younger students can sort cards with pictures, and older students can sort cards with sentences.

7. Objective: Identify the beginning sounds of words.

   Skill Packet: Match plastic letters to pictures of objects.

Skills Development (cont.)

Use pages 101–105 to make worksheets for your Skills Center. Make a copy for each student or pair of students, or glue the worksheet to tagboard and laminate so students can use water-based pens for easy wipe-off and reuse. Here are some ideas.

Abbreviations
Names of states
Days of the week
Units of measurement
Months of the year
blvd. — boulevard
Rd. — road
St. — street
Dr. — drive
Ave. — avenue
Dr. — Doctor
Mrs. — Missus
Mr. — Mister
Gov. — Governor
Pres. — President
mt.— mountain
p. — page
etc. — et cetera
yr. — year
wk. — week

Contractions
isn't — is not
doesn't — does not
haven't — have not
I've — I have
we've — we have
I'm — I am
you're — you are
it's — it is
that's — that is
they'd — they would
I'll — I will
you'll — you will
won't — will not
let's — let us

Compound Words
airplane
anyhow
anything
basketball
bedroom
bodyguard
bookcase
cardboard
classroom
earthquake
everywhere
footnote
grandfather
handwriting
makeup
quarterback
snowflake
suitcase

Plurals
-s	-es	-ies
toe	church	sky
pin	lunch	baby
lamp	box	party
book	brunch	family
kitten	class	cherry
window	inch	body
star	tomato	army
key	waltz	lady

Roman Numerals
I — 1	VI — 6	L — 50
II — 2	VII — 7	C — 100
III — 3	VIII — 8	D — 500
IV — 4	IX — 9	M — 1,000
V — 5	X — 10	

Metric Measurement
mm = millimeter (1/10 cm)
cm = centimeter (10 mm)
dm = decimeter (10 cm)
m = meter (1,000 mm)
km = kilometer (1,000 m)
g = gram
kg = kilogram (1,000 g)
L = liter (1,000 mL)
mL = milliliter
cc = cubic centimeter

Measurement Equivalents
12 in. = 1 ft.
3 ft. = 1 yd.
5,280 ft. = 1 mi.
4 qt. = 1 gal.
2 pt. = 1 qt.
8 oz. = 1 c.
1 T. = 2,000 lbs.
60 sec. = 1 min.
60 min. = 1 hr.

Prefixes
dis-	un-	over-	re-
disapprove	uncut	overcharge	recover
discolor	uneven	overdressed	redo
discount	unfair	overdue	reheat
dislike	unhappy	overfeed	remiss
dismay	unlike	overgrown	replay
dismiss	unmade	overpaid	reset
disobey	unwashed	overrun	review

Suffixes
-ful	-en	-less	-ly
beautiful	harden	ageless	actively
careful	moisten	homeless	happily
helpful	sweeten	priceless	quickly
skillful	thicken	worthless	silently

Synonyms
sleepy — tired	wealthy — rich	friend — pal
firm — solid	quick — fast	tiny — small
story — tale	sea — ocean	jump — leap
shut — close	icy — cold	gift — present
easy — simple	chore — task	hike — walk

Antonyms
empty — full	forget – remember	rough – smooth
tame — wild	thick — slender	light — dark
high — low	sweet — sour	dirty — clean
fast — slow	young — aged	calm — nervous
strong — weak	tall — short	
correct – wrong		

Homonyms
eight — ate	pale — pail	sense — cents — scents
whole — hole	knew — new	
red — read	nose — knows	two — too — to
hour — our	blew — blue	
peace — piece	would — wood	
lone — loan	for – four – fore	

Surprise!

Directions: _____

_____

1.

2.

3.

4.

5.

6.

7.

8.

9.

10.

11.

12.

13.

14.

15.

16.

Answer Bank

Harvest Time

Directions: _____

_____

Answer Bank

Warming Up

Directions: _____

_____

1.

2.

3.

4.

5.

6.

7.

8.

9.

10.

11.

12.

13.

14.

15.

Answer Bank

Up, Up, and Away!

Directions: _____

_____

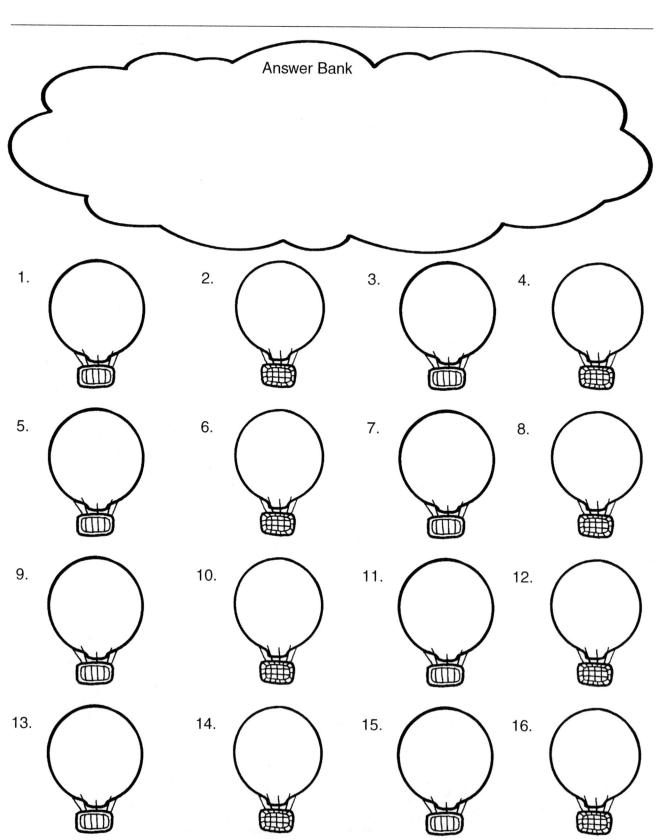

Answer Bank

1.

2.

3.

4.

5.

6.

7.

8.

9.

10.

11.

12.

13.

14.

15.

16.

Does It Compute?

Directions: _____

_____

1.   2.   3.   4.   5.

6.   7.   8.   9.   10.

11.   12.   13.   14.   15.

Answer Bank

File Folder Skills Activities

Materials:

- file folders
- crayons and markers
- wallpaper sample books
- colored adhesive dots

- scissors
- construction paper
- glue or rubber cement

Note: Wallpaper sample books can be obtained from decorating and wallpaper stores. These are valuable resources for making file folder activities, bulletin board letters, and backgrounds, as well as other decorative displays.

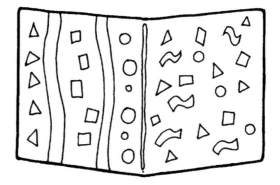

File Folder Activities

Explain to students how to use the file folder activities and how to care for the pieces. You may wish to send these file folder activities home for parents to use with their children.

- Color Matching: Choose a pattern and trace it onto eight pieces of different colored construction paper, making two copies of the pattern out of each color. Cut out the pattern pieces and glue one set onto the inside of a file folder. The other set will be used for matching. Add details to both sets with markers. For durability, laminate the completed file folder and the matching pieces. Place the matching pieces in a resealable plastic bag. Then staple or glue the bag onto the back of the folder.

- Dot Number Matching: Follow the directions described above for cutting and storing the matching pieces. (You may wish to make this activity more difficult by using only one color of construction paper.) Place the same number of adhesive dots on each of two pieces. Glue one set of patterns with the dots onto the file folder. The other set is for matching. The numeral that matches the number of dots may be written on the back of each matching piece.

- Shape Matching: Follow the same general directions as before. Instead of adding dots, use markers to draw shapes (squares, circles, triangles, etc.) on each set of pattern pieces.

- Pattern Matching: Use wallpaper samples to cut two matching pieces. Glue one set of patterns onto the file folder, and the other is for matching. Students match the wallpaper design for each set of patterns. Store the matching pieces as described above.

Wheel Matching

Materials:

- construction paper or poster board
- markers
- scissors
- brad
- compass
- patterns

Directions:

1. Use a compass to draw two circles of different diameters onto construction paper or poster board. See the patterns on page 108 as an example, or reproduce and use the patterns themselves.

2. With a brad, attach the smaller circle to the larger through their centers.

3. Determine the number of items you want students to match and draw the corresponding number of radius lines on both circles.

4. Draw or write the names of the items to be matched on the outer sections of the large circle and the sections of the small circle.

5. Have students turn the circles to match the items.

Some Ideas for Matching:

- colors
- designs
- shapes
- like objects
- like sets
- sets of numerals
- animal families
- parts of speech
- math facts
- science classifications
- cultural connections

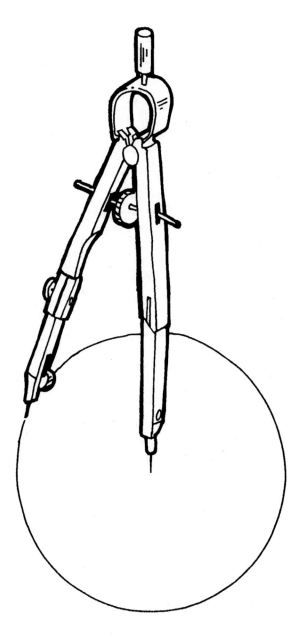

Wheel Matching

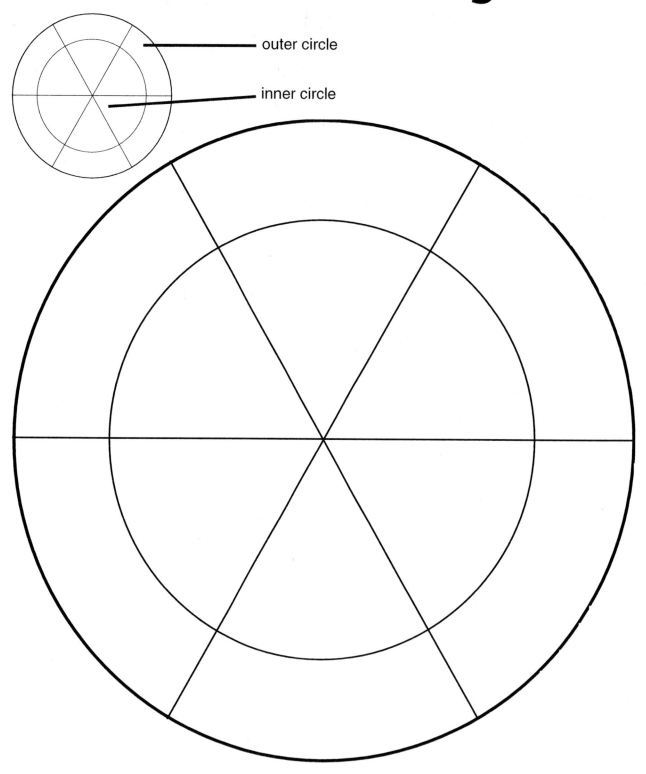

outer circle

inner circle

Clothespin Matching

Materials:

- poster board
- old magazines and catalogs
- scissors
- glue

- spring-clip clothespins
- paint
- crayons or markers

Directions:

1. Decide on a theme and create a montage picture by cutting pictures from magazines.

2. Glue the theme concept picture in the center of a piece of poster board, and glue corresponding pictures around the perimeter. For example, if a farm is the theme, glue a picture of a barn in the center and pictures of various farm animals around the perimeter.

3. Mark a set of clothespins according to the skill you are wishing to reinforce. For the farm example you might write an animal's name on each clothespin.

4. Have students attach the clothespins to the correct pictures.

Some Ideas for Matching:

- colors
- designs
- shapes
- like objects
- like sets

- sets of numerals
- words and pictures
- equal sets
- things that go together
- similar characteristics

Group Centers

Allowing students to choose the classmates they wish to work with respects their right to make choices, but it can also limit social interactions and student progress and make classroom management extremely difficult. For that reason, most teachers assign students to particular groups while allowing for variation. For example, you may wish to allow students to work with whomever they choose yet meet with you in different assigned groups.

Students can rotate through all of the centers in the same groupings, but this often creates behavior problems because students are consistently working with the same peers. An alternate suggestion is to complete center rotations on a daily basis and change group members each day. Before beginning Centers time, draw names out of a hat, call names, or accept volunteers to form each center's group. Then rotate the groups at the scheduled times.

Students usually enjoy working with different classmates each day. You may wish to group them by interest, ability, need, or learning style. Yet another option is to group students on a weekly basis and have them complete one center rotation together each day. Below is a sample plan you may wish to re-create and use to help you form groups according to achievement level and special needs. Depending on your needs, these variables can change. For example, some centers may be based on student needs, while others attempt to capitalize on students' talents or take into consideration gender, interest, ability, and attitude.

Selecting Cooperative Groups

HA: High Achiever
SN: Special Needs Student
ESL: English as a Second Language Student
CA: Competent Achiever

Group One (example)	**Group Two**	**Group Three**
(HA)	( )	( )
(CA)	( )	( )
(CA)	( )	( )
(SN)	( )	( )
(ESL)	( )	( )
Notes: _____	Notes: _____	Notes: _____
_____	_____	_____
_____	_____	_____

Group Four	**Group Five**	**Group Six**
( )	( )	( )
( )	( )	( )
( )	( )	( )
( )	( )	( )
( )	( )	( )
Notes: _____	Notes: _____	Notes: _____
_____	_____	_____
_____	_____	_____

How to Create New Centers

You can let your imagination and the needs of your students help you create your own learning center activities.

1. Select a theme or topic. Label the center attractively with a display or poster. (Example: birds)

2. Determine specific skills or concepts to be taught or reinforced. (birds, nests, feathers, eggs)

3. Choose appropriate learning activities areas. (life cycle; incubation; matching birds with feathers, nest, eggs)

4. Prepare extended activities for reinforcement or enrichment. (worksheets, art activities, binoculars, creative writing, poems)

5. Gather necessary materials.

Use Bloom's Taxonomy as a base. Structure your center's activities around the six levels of thinking:

a. Knowledge—learning

b. Comprehension—understanding what is learned

c. Application—using acquired and understood information

d. Analysis—examining information

e. Synthesis—reacting to learning

f. Evaluation—judging and reviewing information

You may wish to use the form on page 112 to help you organize your thoughts, materials, and activities as you create a new center.

How to Create New Centers (cont.)

Level: _____

_____

_____

Literature: _____

_____

_____

Author: _____

_____

Illustrator: _____

_____

Publisher: _____

_____

Purpose: _____

_____

Materials: _____

_____

Preparation: _____

_____

Instructions: _____

_____

Suggested Curriculum Centers

 **Listening Center**—cassettes, records, or radio for students to listen and respond (by drawing, writing, worksheet, etc.)

 **Reading Center**—wide variety of reading materials (magazines, books, newspaper articles, etc.) and related skills activities

 **Library Center**—collection of 200-300 books, fiction and nonfiction, commercially published and student-made, with follow-up activities; closely linked to the Reading Center

 Writing Center—journal, report, prompt-generated, or free writing; vocabulary charts; student-made books for other students to read

 Math Center—materials (manipulatives and written activities) for sorting, counting, grouping, sequencing, or practicing other math skills

 Science Center—experiments, observations, reading, worksheets, use of equipment (microscope, magnifying glass, etc.)

 Social Studies Center—fiction and nonfiction books, reference materials, and maps describing the world, different communities, and people's social structures and interactions

 **Research Center**—dictionary, thesaurus, encyclopedia, atlas, with activities that encourage asking questions and finding the answers

 **Computer Center**—computer, software, and printer to encourage exploration and technological literacy

 Art Center—special projects, holiday or monthly theme ideas, variety of media (clay, water colors, toothpicks, etc.), or projects linked to the curriculum

 **Puzzles and Games Center**—teacher- or student-made games, electronic games, puzzles, word searches, crossword puzzles, etc.

 **Hands-On Center**—experiencing the manipulation of many different materials, allowing for student growth in several areas of development

Drama Center—opportunities for oral expression; equipped with hats, props, masks, and costumes, as well as other useful materials such as scripts and puppets

Listening Centers

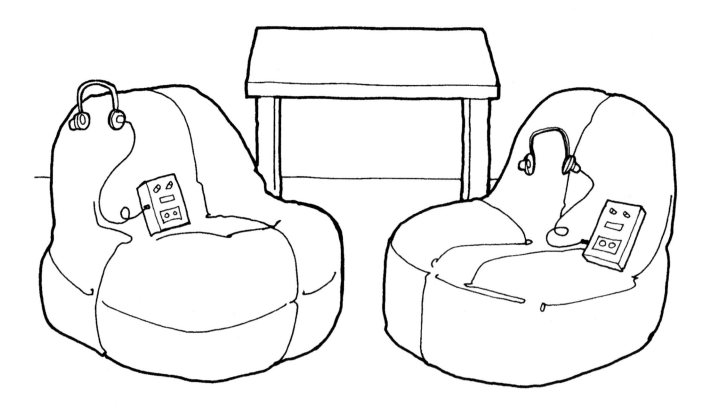

Listening Centers (cont.)

Stepping Into Literacy

The Listening Center may be the most important center in your classroom. Seize every opportunity to acquire books with corresponding cassette tapes. It is best to have at least two copies of the book to go with each tape. Work toward obtaining multiple copies of the very best books. The Listening Center can be combined with an Author and/or Music Center to make a megacenter. The opportunity to hear stories read aloud is essential for literacy.

The Value of Repetition

Most children love to hear their favorite books and stories read again and again. Some of your students may lack the listening experience essential for reading success. While such deficiencies are difficult to overcome, a library of tapes will go a long way to remediate the problem. Students can listen to the same tapes over and over while following along in the books. Working in pairs seems to stimulate learning as children assist each other and share the experience. Students like to memorize books and read along, an important first step to literacy. Blank tapes can be provided so fluent readers can make tapes to add more stories to the library in the Listening Center.

Motivating Students

To stimulate interest in a new book and/or a tape added to the center, read the book aloud to the class. Magnetic board characters, dolls, or activities that go with the story also encourage children to get heavily involved in the story and want to experience it repeatedly. Use the shared-reading or after-lunch read-aloud time to build motivation. Occasionally have students respond to a book or story with creating related artwork. Play the tape or read the story aloud as they create. Store the books and corresponding tapes separately to encourage students to read titles and labels and match them up.

Training Students How to Use the Equipment

Plan to have several training lessons on how to use the tape recorder, headphones, and reading/listening materials correctly. Find a tape recorder that is especially designed for student use—sturdy and easy to operate. You may wish to stick colored dots above the buttons on the recorder to help nonreaders. Use green for play, red for stop, orange for rewind, yellow for pause, and blue for fast-forward. Also clearly mark a volume limit line. Model for the class proper use of the equipment and explain the color code.

Listening Centers (cont.)

Preventing Tape Erasures or Tape-overs

To prevent students from erasing recorded tapes, break off the little tabs on the backs of the cassettes. If at a later time you wish to record over a tape, cover the holes in the back of the cassette with tape. Tapes break, so be sure to make back-up copies of all your tapes.

Headphones—Pros and Cons

Headphones reduce noise in the classroom, but you must decide whether this is what you want or not. Using headphones may inhibit the cooperative experience of students singing and/or reading together. If headphones are used, you cannot hear the selection the student has chosen. Students often impulsively sing or read along, and if not accompanied by the music their voices will seem loud and distracting.

The Hidden Benefits of Music

Students can get a great deal of reading instruction and/or reinforcement by reading along while listening to songs. Make charts of the lyrics to familiar songs so students can read as they sing along to the music. Place laminated copies of song lyrics in a class scrapbook in the Listening Center. Be sure that the lyrics are very easy to read. Have students using the Art Center create pictures to laminate with the lyrics.

Special Tapes

Some students may need modified materials in order to be successful. Tapes often move too fast for beginners to match spoken words with printed ones. Choose some easy books and record them as you read at a slower pace. To get an idea of the correct oral reading tempo, touch each word of the text with your finger as you record the story. Encourage students to follow along in the book by pointing to each word as it is read.

Where to Begin

Student interest is the most important factor to consider when choosing books and tapes. Scholastic and Troll book clubs usually have a good selection of matching books and tapes. Check with local music stores and children's bookstores to expand your collection.

Listening Center Model

Your students know a lot about what it means to be a friend. Here is an exciting and unusual way for them to show what they have learned about friendship. Follow the steps with your class and let students experience the fun of creating their own listening center.

Step One: Discuss the parts of a listening center: cassette tape recorder, cassette tape, headphones, and books with text to match words on the tape.

Step Two: Explain that as a class they are going to create a listening center.

Step Three: Review what students have learned about friendship by brainstorming and writing their responses on chart paper.

We are all friends. Friends can be different. We have fun with our friends. We help friends. Friends can be different people or animals. Some friends are like me. Friends help us.

Step Four: Using the chart as a guide, have students come up with the text for listening center booklets. Write out the sentences on sentence strips. Read them with the class. Example:

We are friends.

Friends are different.

It is okay to be different.

Friends help each other.

Step Five: Gather students and have them practice reading the sentence strips aloud together slowly and clearly.

Step Six: Record the students reading the text. Begin by having the class say, "Let's Be Friends...written, illustrated, and recorded by (teacher's) (grade) class." Then have the class read aloud each sentence. Assign one student to give an audible signal (such as ringing a bell) to tell students when to go to the next page.

Listening Center Model *(cont.)*

Step Seven: Play back the tape for all to hear. Brainstorm with the class about how they want to illustrate the pages of their listening center read-along booklets.

Step Eight: Copy each sentence near the bottom of five full-sized pieces of paper to create five separate "Let's Be Friends" booklets.

Examples:

Page 3	Page 4
It is okay to be different.	Friends help each other.

Step Nine: Distribute the pages for students to illustrate. Add a cover to each book and have students write the title and illustrate the covers, or reproduce page 119 and have students color it. (Be sure to white-out or turn under the printed text on the top of the page before reproducing.)

Step Ten: Collate the pages and the cover to create five "Let's Be Friends" booklets. Staple the pages along the left edge and cover the staples with tape.

Step Eleven: Create a listening center in your classroom with a sign that says, "Come and listen with a friend!" Put the class books and tape in the center.

Step Twelve: Share the fun with another class by inviting them to come visit your Listening Center, or lend them your student-created tape and booklets to enjoy in their classroom. Reproduce and use the sample invitation on page 120. Have your class serve refreshments and treat their guests as friends.

Listening Center Model (cont.)

Let's Be Friends

by _____

Invitation

Hello, Friends!

We would like to invite you to share a book and tape about friendship at our new Listening Center. Please come to our class on _____ at _____. Refreshments will be served. See you there!

_____ Class

Reading Centers

Reading Centers (cont.)

As students practice their reading skills, they often mimic what they have already experienced, which means they often play school. Be sure the center has small chalkboards, charts, pointers, big books, and instructional and writing materials. If the children have not played school by midterm, model the activity and set up a pretend school.

For younger students, especially kindergarteners, emphasis should be on concrete materials and on process. You can expect older students to produce projects and complete activities that you can assess and use to document their progress.

Equipment:

- chalkboard, chalk, and erasers
- large magnetic board or metal file cabinet
- bookshelf or book display
- stapler
- shelves
- comfortable chair
- table or desk

Materials:

- word cards, at least one set with pictures
- alphabet blocks
- teacher-made blank booklets
- blank word cards and sentence strips
- scrap box
- easy readers
- magnetic board (or large cookie sheets)
- magnetic letters and story characters
- crossword puzzles
- spelling games
- Rebus stories and charts
- sequence cards of popular stories
- alphabet poster
- filmstrips
- commercial reading kits
- letter tiles (upper-case set and lower-case set)
- placemats with alphabet letters and matching pictures
- commercial and handmade reading games
- large variety of books, including those written by children
- battery operated, hand-held computer games

Reading Centers (cont.)

Activities:

- reading silently

- reading aloud in a group or with partners

- listening to a story tape and completing a sequencing activity

- book reviews (pages 124–125)

- writing endings to stories

- writing in a reader's response journal (page 126)

- working with the alphabet (pages 127–129)

- reading aloud in a group and predicting

- consonant, vowel, and blend activities

- prefix and suffix activities (pages 130–132)

- root word activities

- contraction activities

- synonym, antonym, and homonym activities

- rhyming activities

- comprehension activities

- magnetic letter manipulation

- poetry readings (student and published)

Book Review—A

Name _____

Book Title _____

Author _____

Why I liked this book:

    1. _____

    2. _____

    3. _____

    4. _____

Why I did not like this book:

    1. _____

    2. _____

    3. _____

    4. _____

Circle your choices and explain your opinions.

Why I think other students in this class will / will not like this book.

_____

_____

_____

_____

Why I think younger / older children will like this book.

_____

_____

_____

_____

Book Review—B

Name _____

Book Title _____

Author _____

Number of pages _____

Topic or Theme _____

1. I chose to read this book because _____

2. The story is about _____

3. I rate this book as exciting / interesting / boring / okay _____

   because _____

5. My favorite thing about the book is _____

6. What I did not like about the book is _____

Reader's Response Journal

Name		
Book Title		
Quote	**Chapter, Page**	**My Thoughts**

Alphabet/Alliteration Activities Area

An area containing manipulatives and activities involving letters and sounds is necessary in every primary whole language classroom. Children who have not reached the level of taking words apart into letters and sounds will be afforded the opportunity to practice these important skills. Students who have mastered letters and sounds will enjoy and extend these activities that "play" with our language. This type of area is also especially effective for ESL (English as a Second Language) students.

Make available several alphabet, alliterative, and word books for students to use.

Sets of individual alphabet letters and/or pictures with accompanying letters can be purchased. Or you can make them by cutting apart appropriate posters or books, such as *David McPhail's Alphabet Book A to Z* (Scholastic, 1989). Note: If you choose to cut up alphabet books to make individual cards, you'll need to have two books so you can cut out both sides of the back-to-back pages. Glue these on construction paper so that students are not confused as to which side to use. Lamination increases durability.

Be sure to provide a more challenging set where no letter is displayed and the student must identify the letter by using the picture clue only. Here are some alphabet tasks you can encourage students to use. They will invent many more on their own.

- Put the letters in alphabetical order.

- "Walk" the letters by placing them on the floor and then identifying and stepping on each. Students can name the letter, picture, or another word that has that letter at the beginning or end.

- After putting the letters in alphabetical order, play "missing letter" with other students. One student takes out a letter while other players turn away or cover their eyes. Then players are asked to open their eyes and identify the missing letter.

- Purchase magnetic letters and provide these for students to manipulate. These letters can be used on the side of a file cabinet or on large metal cookie sheets. These areas need to be large enough for more than one student to work.

- Provide word cards with phonetic words, high frequency words, or "theme" words for students to write with magnetic letters and read.

- The same kind of activities listed above can be done using individual letter stamps and ink pads.

Upper-case Alphabet

A	B	C	D
E	F	G	H
I	J	K	L
M	N	O	P
Q	R	S	T
U	V	W	X
Y	Z		

Lower-case Alphabet

a	b	c	d
e	f	g	h
i	j	k	l
m	n	o	p
q	r	s	t
u	v	w	x
y	z		

Reading Center Model

Activity:

Prefix Train

Skill:

Recognizing and using prefixes

Objective:

To add a prefix to a root word to make a new word

Materials:

- poster board, tagboard, or file folder
- string-tie envelope
- markers or colored pencils
- scissors
- glue
- patterns
- answer key

Directions:

1. Reproduce page 131 and glue it on one side of a piece of poster board, tagboard, or file folder.
2. Use a marker to darken the words "Example" and "Hint" and the prefix on the train and in the sample words.
3. Reproduce page 132 and glue the boxcar page next to the example/directions page.
4. Reproduce and cut out the wheel word cards (page 133). Glue them onto poster board or tagboard and cut them out.
5. Create an answer key by reproducing pages 132 and 133 and cutting out and gluing the wheels on the correct boxcar. Mount the answer key on a separate piece of poster board or tagboard. (Answer Key: unable, unhappy, disappear, disarm, enrage, enclose, submarine, subway, preview, precook, inside, invisible, impolite, impossible, misbehave, mismatch, rewrite, repay)
6. Label a string-tie envelope "Prefix Train" and store the wheel word cards and the answer key in it.

Additional Activities:

1. Invite students to work with partners. Have them write sentences in pairs to show how prefixes change the meaning of words.
2. After students have correctly matched all the words to prefixes in the center, have them use the words in sentences. Students can first use each word in a sentence without the prefix added and then with the prefix. Allow students to use dictionaries to help identify word meanings.
3. Encourage students to pretend that they are prefix "explorers." Provide them with copies of a short story, page from a book, or other passage at the appropriate reading level. Give students markers and ask them to find and circle words that have a prefix. Then have students write a list of the words they circled.

Reading Center Model *(cont.)*

Directions: Get the train ready to run by correctly putting the wheels on the boxcars.

1. Read the Hint.

2. Take the wheel word cards out of the envelope.

3. Find two wheel word cards that go with the prefix on each boxcar. Place them on the boxcar wheels. See if you can get wheel word cards on all the boxcars.

Example:

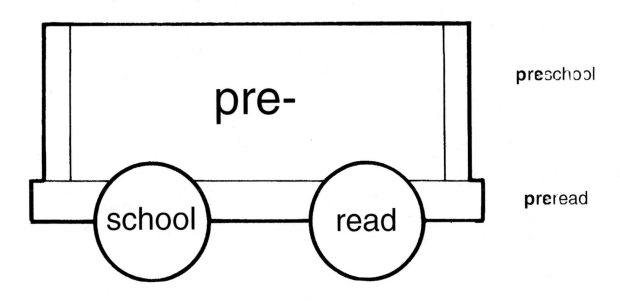

4. When you have finished, use the answer key to check your work.

Hint: A prefix is a group of letters added to the beginning of a root word. It changes the meaning of the root word. (Example: build—rebuild)

Some prefixes and their meanings:

dis— not	pre—before	im—not
en—became	mis—not	sub—under
in—not	re—to do again	un—not

Reading Center Model (cont.)

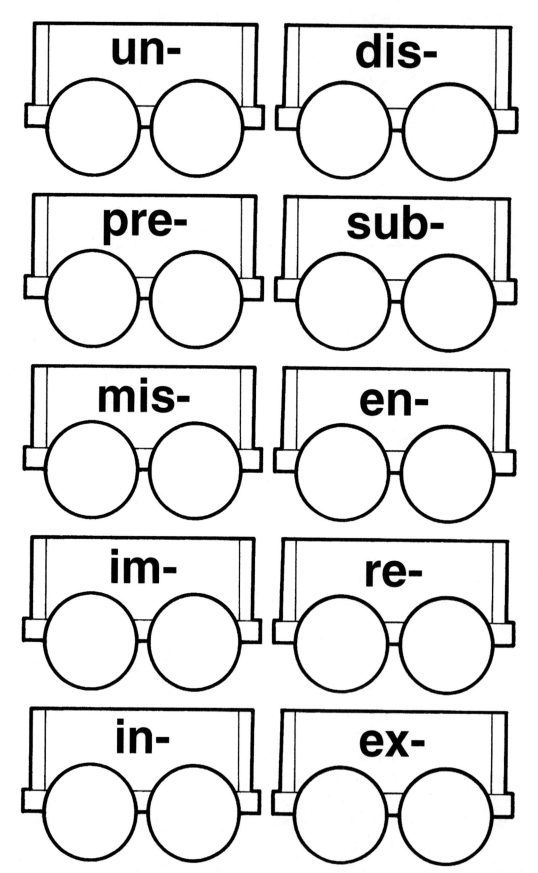

un-   dis-

pre-   sub-

mis-   en-

im-   re-

in-   ex-

Reading Center Model *(cont.)*

able

appear

rage

marine

view

side

polite

behave

happy

write

arm

close

way

cook

visible

possible

match

pay

Library Centers

Combining Centers to Create a Megacenter

The Library Center can be combined with other centers to create a megacenter and give students a greater choice of activities. Books should be changed about every four to six weeks. It is very important to try to coordinate book selection with other activities taking place in the room and also with the current season or an upcoming holiday.

- **Library/Reading or Library/Listening Center**

  Be sure to include some easy reader books. Provide two or more copies of each book. Books can and should be everywhere in the classroom and in all of the centers.

- **Library/Drama Center**

  If these two centers are combined, there should be a puppet stage and materials to make puppets and write plays. Students can write plays in which they are the characters and create costumes and props for the drama. Provide flannel board and felt pieces and have students write stories and act out the stories on the flannel board. Be sure to provide a table for students to work at in this center.

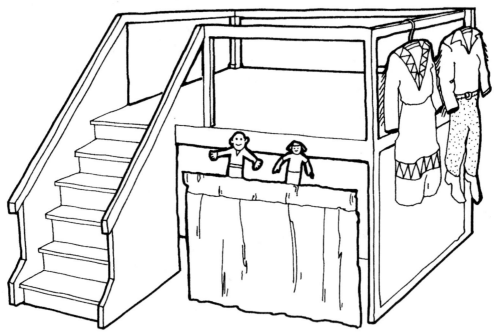

Leisure Reading

Leisure reading materials should be available for students during extra time as well as during assigned periods of silent reading. Students learn to read by reading, and many teachers have success with a daily period of silent reading when everyone, including the teacher, reads.

Gathering books for leisure reading can be accomplished in several ways. Students can be encouraged to bring books to school to read. Take class field trips to your school library and let students pick out a book. Ask friends and parents to donate books to the classroom. (Be sure to read them first to check that they are appropriate for public school and your class.) Many districts require that books used in the classroom go through an evaluation process and be on an approved list. Check with your district.

Library Center Model

While the Library Center is used primarily for choosing and reading books, activities such as the following can also be used.

Level: Kindergarten

Literature: *Brown Bear, Brown Bear, What Do You See?*

Author: Bill Martin, Jr.

Illustrator: Eric Carle

Publisher: Henry Holt and Company, New York, 1983

Purpose: To provide a center that focuses on a book for beginning readers

Materials:

- at least 1 copy of the literature selection
- 2 pattern sheets for each student (pages 136 and 137)
- 1 language sheet for each student (page 138)
- crayons
- scissors
- glue

Preparation:

Reproduce the patterns and language sheets. Make a chart with the instructions for the activity. Use learning center signs to show students how to cut and paste the patterns on the language sheets. Make a sample for students to see.

Instructions:

Familiarize students with the book by reading it aloud to the class or having an adult or older student volunteer read it to students at the center. Discuss the language patterns. Have students re-create the first verses of the story using the patterns and language sheet. Students should be able to read the verses back to you, using the pictures and basic language.

Library Center Model (cont.)

Patterns

Library Center Model (cont.)

Patterns

Library Center Model (cont.)

Language Sheet

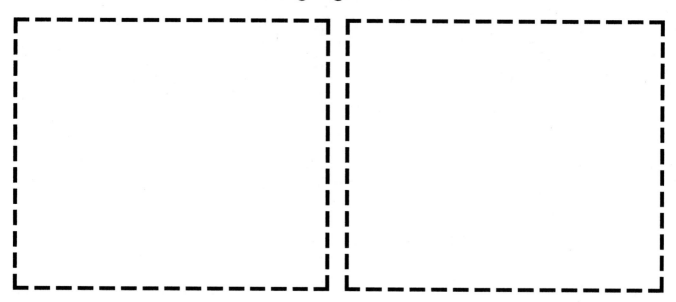

What do you see?

I see a

looking at me.

Writing Centers

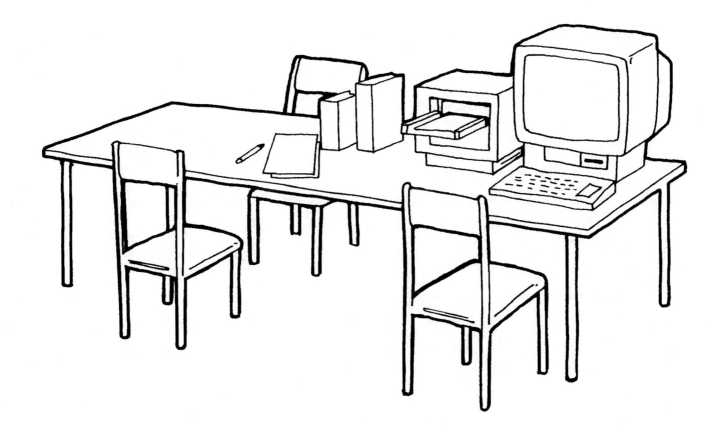

Writing Centers *(cont.)*

Suggestions

- Students may write their own versions of a story, following the same pattern but inserting their own word choices.

- Make booklets of students' stories.

- Provide a story frame for students, with blanks for color and animal words.

- Work in writing journals. Prompts are provided on page 142.

- Work with partners to write a mystery, science fiction thriller, fairy tale, comic book, or other story.

- Write poetry.

- Write song lyrics.

- Write new lyrics to familiar songs.

- Write letters to friends.

- Keep a post office, where students write postcards, notes, or letters to each other and then deliver them to mailboxes set up for each student, the teacher, the principal, and others. Shoe boxes make wonderful mailboxes.

- Rewrite the endings to familiar stories.

- Write familiar stories from the perspective of the story's antagonist (villain).

- Write a story based on a famous artwork or a picture from a magazine.

- Choose ten words randomly from the dictionary or a list of vocabulary words and incorporate them into a story.

- In groups, write stories one sentence at a time, person by person.

- Write sentence parallels. For example, "She ate a red apple" can be changed to "He wrote an interesting letter" or "They climbed the tallest tree."

- Write showing (descriptive) paragraphs from telling sentences.

- Publish books. Refer to pages 143–144.

- Diagram sentences.

- Write, design, and make product packages for imaginary or real products.

- Write and design advertisements for imaginary products.

- Write scripts from familiar stories or original ones.

- Write and design dust jackets for favorite books.

- Write letters to companies either supporting or criticizing what they do.

- Write modern fables that use traditional proverbs or morals.

- Provide copies of the sample writing paper (pages 145–148) for students to use at the center.

Writing Centers *(cont.)*

Writer's Box

Each student should have his or her own Writer's Box in which to store writings (completed and/or in progress). Use large empty cereal boxes with their tops cut off and their wide sides cut at a slant. Cover the boxes with colorful contact paper or let each student decorate his/her box and label it with his/her name.

Writer's Workshop Resource Center

There should be one location that contains all writing "props," but this does not mean it is the only location of these items. Many items should be duplicated and placed in various centers and areas around the room. Also, do not put out every writing prop at one time. When you observe children are weary of certain items, introduce, delete, or change some of them.

Instruments	**Materials**	**Electives**	**References**
• variety of pens • thin and wide crayons and pencils • bold and pastel colored pencils • bold and pastel colored chalk in various sizes and thicknesses • bold and pastel colored markers in various tip sizes • individual Writer's Boxes (see above) If Available: • tape recorders • typewriters • instamatic cameras • computers • class mailboxes	• all types of paper • paper stapled to make small blank books • note pads, memo pads, self-sticking pads • all shapes, sizes, and colors of envelopes • canceled stamps, stickers, address labels • junk mail • variety of adhesive tape, glue sticks, glue, paste, staplers, hole punches, paper clips, erasers, brad fasteners, yarn, string, pipe cleaners	• paints and a variety of paintbrushes • variety of rubber stamps and ink pads in a variety of colors • laminated lists (alphabet numbers, words, children's names) • mini dry erase boards with wipe-a-way markers • mini chalkboards • clipboards • sandpaper • flannel boards • play clay • glitter • dry pasta letters and numbers • letter, number and picture stencils • magnetic board with letters/numbers	• literature books of all kinds (fiction, nonfiction; no text, lots of text; variety of illustration mediums) • dictionaries, variety of levels • telephone books • restaurant menus • maps and globes • mail-order catalogs • magazines, all types and reading levels • newspapers • comic books • old calendars • student-made books • writing wall of words, symbols, and phrases

Writing Prompts

The most interesting thing about me is . . .

What I like best about my friend _____ is . . .

I am the one who . . .

The earth is a wonderful place . . .

The greatest day I ever had was . . .

Something I am glad to know about is . . .

If I had three wishes . . .

The day the Martians landed . . .

I was so surprised when I woke up to find . . .

The strangest thing I ever saw was . . .

I passed by the pet store on my way to school, and in the window I saw . . .

If I ran the school I would . . .

You may not believe it, but last week my parents put me in charge of the house and I . . .

If I could travel inside a book, I would . . .

If I became invisible I would . . .

If I woke up as my brother or sister I would . . .

Publishing Company

Publishing student-authored books is highly effective in boosting students' confidence as writers. It also makes the writing process relevant in students' lives because they realize that authors are real people and that they themselves are capable of being authors.

Set up a publishing company that can be used continuously with little maintenance. Choose a location in your classroom with a small partition for displaying a Publishing Company sign (a small bulletin board or poster). Be sure the location has ample counter or table space for the following:

- a supply of premade blank books for publishing (directions on page 144)
- receptacles for crayons, colored pencils, markers, pastels, and letter stencils or rub-on letters for titles (to be used as publishing supplies only)
- space to display already published books
- space for references books such as dictionaries (at all levels), word books, thesaurus, etc.

Publishing Company *(cont.)*

Obtain manuscripts (stories) for publishing from student journal entries or creative writing assignments. Be sure that all students at all ability levels periodically publish a book.

For ESL and other students who may need more help, take dictation. As the student reads his or her work to you, you print it in the blank book. Be sure to repeat what they say so you keep the intent of the story intact, but correct grammar and word usage as you repeat their ideas. Allow the student to watch you as you spell, punctuate, and read the words you write. Guide the student in choosing an appropriate title for the book, and write it on the cover. Have the student read the book to you, then illustrate the pages.

Making a Blank Book for Publishing

Materials:

- 9" x 12" (22 cm x 30 cm) piece of construction paper
- 3 or 4 pieces of 8 ½" by 11" (21 cm x 28 cm) paper
- stapler
- book tape or colored plastic tape about 2" (5 cm) wide

Directions:

1. Fold the piece of construction paper in half.
2. Fold the sheets of writing paper in half.
3. Place the open ends of the writing papers in the fold of the construction paper.
4. Staple along the outside edge of the fold to create the book binding.
5. Tape over the staples.

Ways We Travel

Writing Paper A

Name _____

Writing Paper B

Name _____

Writing Paper C

A B C D E F

Z Name _____

_____

G

Y -

_____

H

X _____

I

W -

_____

J

V -

K

U _____

L

T -

_____

M

S R Q P O N

Writing Paper D

Name _____

Student/Teacher Writing Conference Report

Student's Name _____

1. What is the student's attitude toward the piece?

   _____

   _____

2. What is the student's reaction when he or she sees or hears a miscue in the story?

   _____

   _____

3. Do miscues reveal signs of growth such as movement toward convention?

   _____

   _____

4. Does the student ask questions about conventions?

   _____

   _____

5. Does the student reveal or correct language during use?

   _____

   _____

6. What type of changes does the student make when revising or self-correcting?

   _____

   _____

Additional comments:

_____

_____

_____

_____

Peer Writing Conference Report

Writer's Name _____

Partner's Name _____

Process

1. The partner reads the writing.

2. The writer talks about the writing and asks questions.

3. The partner comments and offers suggestions to the writer to assist in the revision process.

4. The partner completes the conference form.

Peer Feedback

1. What I like about the writing is..._____

   _____

   _____

2. My favorite part of your writing is..._____

   _____

   _____

3. What confuses me in the writing is... _____

   _____

   _____

4. I'd like to know more about...in your writing._____

   _____

   _____

Story Map

Goldilocks Story Map

There were three bowls of porridge on the table.

One was too hot.   One was too cold.   But one was just right, so she ate it.

She saw a cute cottage.

She went inside.

Then she saw three chairs.

Goldilocks went for a walk in the woods.

Directions:

On a separate sheet of paper, make a map of a book you have read.

1. Draw pictures of the important events in your story.

2. Write about each picture.

3. Color the pictures.

4. Cut the pictures out and glue them to a large sheet of paper.

5. Draw arrows to make a path from one picture to the next.

6. Share your map with a friend. See if he or she can understand the basic plot of your story.

Math Centers

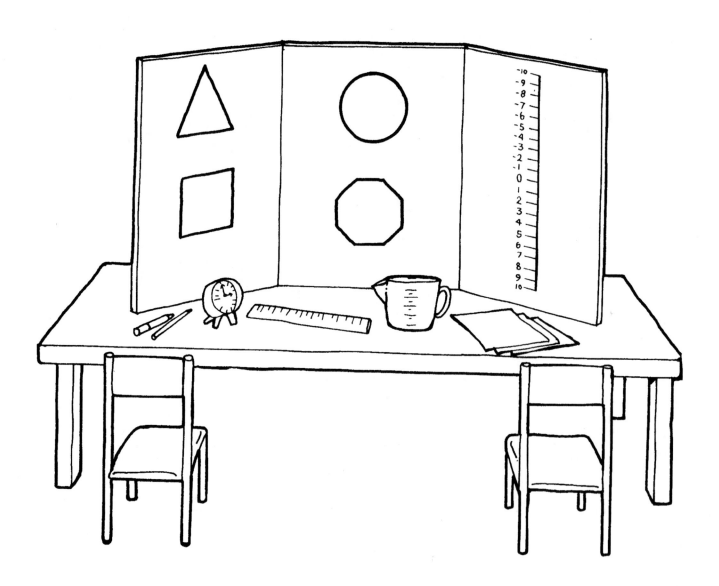

Planning for Center-Based Math

Math centers require a large amount of materials, so you may wish to combine centers or establish specific math theme centers that you can change throughout the year. Placing math and science together reinforces the math/science connection, which is essential to the future of a technological society. Math/Blocks Centers work together to teach number concepts, sorting, and geometry skills. Math can be combined in the Drama Center to illustrate to students how math relates to real-life in areas such as shopping (money) and cooking (measurement).

Suggested Materials for Math Megacenters

Number Concepts—Theme Center or Math/ Blocks Megacenter

- craft sticks
- counting cubes
- buttons
- numeral cards
- rocks for counting
- plastic teddy bears or other animal counters
- clothespins with numerals written on them
- counting games
- fraction manipulatives and related games
- plastic links and activity cards
- teacher-made number dot cards
- teacher-made containers with numerals

Measurement —Theme Center, Math/Science or Math/Drama Megacenters

- large working clock model; small clocks for students
- clock stamp
- pictures of activities symbolizing different times of day
- tapes and books about telling time
- coin stamps (heads and tails)
- blank booklets for money and time activities
- tape measure
- scales, two kinds
- interlocking cubes
- plastic measuring cups and spoons; empty plastic containers
- rulers, yardsticks, metersticks

Suggested Materials for Math Megacenters *(cont.)*

Problem Solving— Math Center. Activities include: classifying and sorting, patterning, graphing, word problems, and creating problems.

- dominoes
- paper scraps
- graph paper
- empty, transparent plastic containers
- blank calendars and sheets of numerals
- nesting blocks
- pattern blocks and activity cards

- materials for sorting: lids, nature objects, toys, shells, plastic shapes, paper, sorting grids, counting sticks, plastic animals, plastic beans
- attribute blocks
- sentence strips
- blank word cards

Geometry—Theme Center or Math/Blocks Center

- blocks
- linking cubes
- plastic or wood tangrams
- shape templates/stencils
- attribute blocks or other plastic shapes of various colors

- geometric models of a cube, sphere, cone, cylinder, rectangular prism, and triangular prism
- geoboards and rubber bands
- parquetry

Applications—Math/Drama Megacenter. Students are very adept creating their own dramatic play ideas. Be sure to brainstorm ideas with the class, and change the center's focus throughout the year. Some ideas with some suggested materials are listed below.

- restaurant—menus, order pads, cash register
- grocery store—tags, labels, scales, play food
- space center or rocket ship—computer, barometer, thermometer

- toy store—tags, toys, receipts, bags
- home kitchen—no-cook recipes and measuring supplies
- table games and activities

Operations—Place these materials in several centers to provide math support where needed.

- calculators
- interlocking cubes
- story boards (made by students or teachers)
- flannel boards or carpet samples
- felt figures: shapes, butterflies, zoo animals (theme related)
- regular paper, large stiff paper, graph paper
- precut paper shapes

- paper number lines
- dice with dots, dice with numerals
- game spinners
- blank teacher- or student-made books
- addition and subtraction flash cards and games
- other manipulatives such as buttons, rocks, animal counters, shells

Manipulatives

Math manipulatives are any objects that students can handle to help them solve math problems. Manipulatives help students visualize what math functions mean. For example, when learning addition, students could combine sets of erasers rather than abstractly adding numerals on paper. Using manipulatives establishes concrete learning in preparation for more abstract learning. Using a variety of manipulatives also adds interest to a lesson and helps students learn that math can be fun.

Measurement—(all in metric and standard measurements) rulers, yardsticks, meter sticks, measuring tape, measuring cups, scales

Computation—calculators, fact charts (multiplication, etc.); variety of manipulatives to illustrate units (ones, tens, hundreds)

Place Value—collections of objects in ones, tens, and hundreds bundles; place value chart

Geometry—flat and three-dimensional items in basic shapes

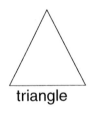 pyramid 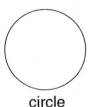 sphere 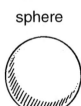 cube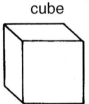

triangle   circle   square

Money—play money: coins and bills

Time—small clocks with movable hands; digital clocks; clocks with Roman numerals

   3 : 00 AM

Fractions and Decimals—fraction kits

 1/4   1/2    .75

Basic Numbers 0-10

0	1	2
3	4	5
6	7	8
9	10	

Counting Numbers 1-100

1	2	3	4	5	6	7	8	9	10
11	12	13	14	15	16	17	18	19	20
21	22	23	24	25	26	27	28	29	30
31	32	33	34	35	36	37	38	39	40
41	42	43	44	45	46	47	48	49	50
51	52	53	54	55	56	57	58	59	60
61	62	63	64	65	66	67	68	69	70
71	72	73	74	75	76	77	78	79	80
81	82	83	84	85	86	87	88	89	90
91	92	93	94	95	96	97	98	99	100

Time

Reproduce, color, laminate, and cut out. Affix the hands at the clock center with a brad.

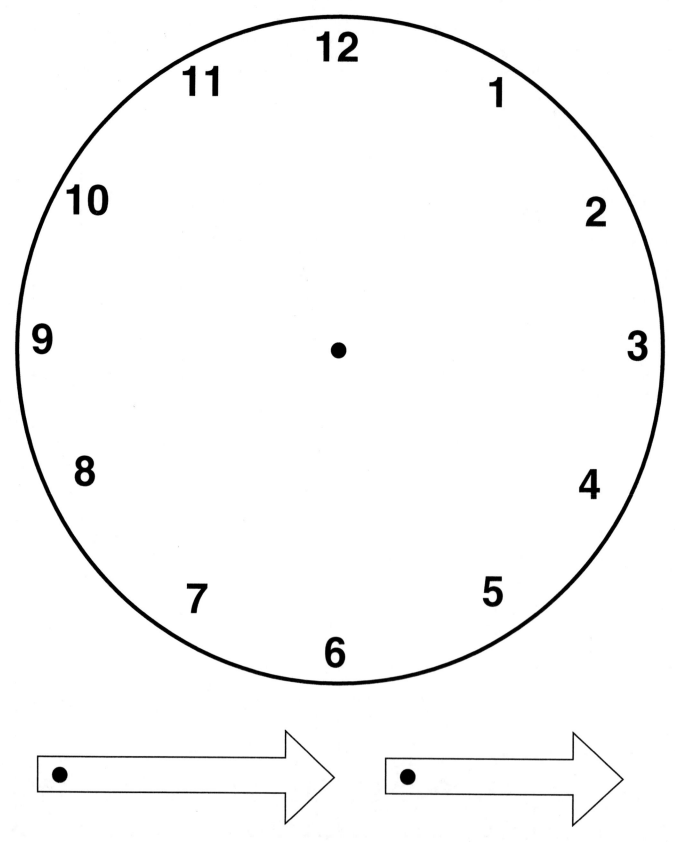

© *Teacher Created Resources, Inc.*

Money—Coins

Reproduce, color, laminate, and cut out.

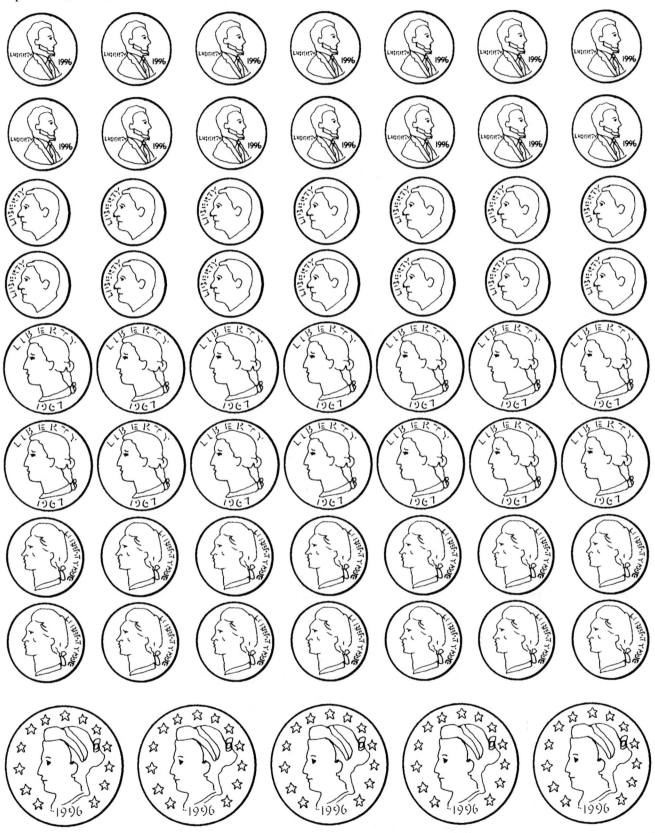

Money—Bills

Reproduce, color, laminate, and cut out.

Base Ten Block Patterns

Use this page to make base ten transparencies and/or homemade base ten blocks. Reproduce, color, laminate, and cut out.

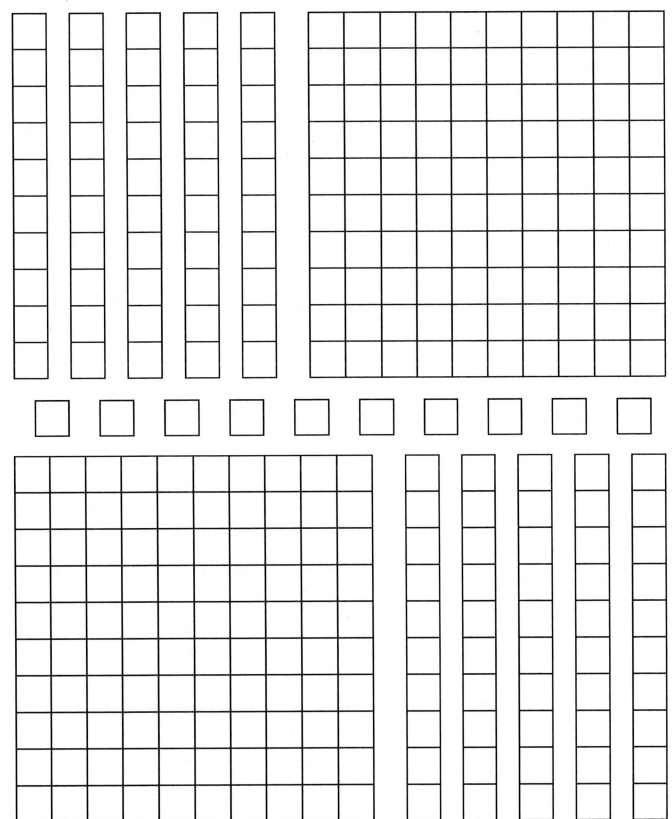

Inch Graph

Reproduce and use intact or cut into strips and squares for open-ended math projects such as graphs, number stairs, arrays, and operations.

Centimeter Graph

Reproduce and use intact or cut into strips and squares for open-ended math projects such as graphs, number stairs, arrays, and operations.

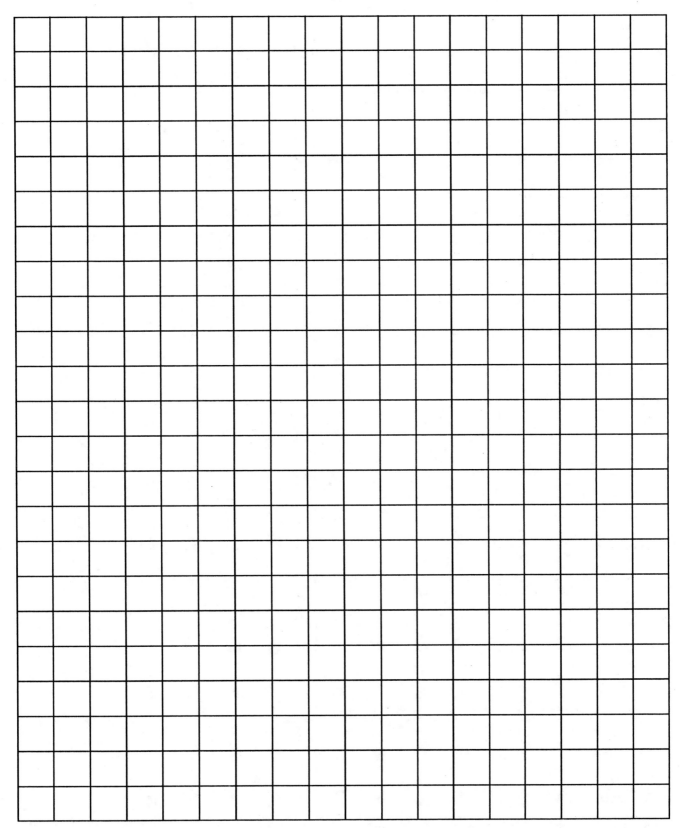

Domino Patterns

Reproduce, laminate, and cut out.

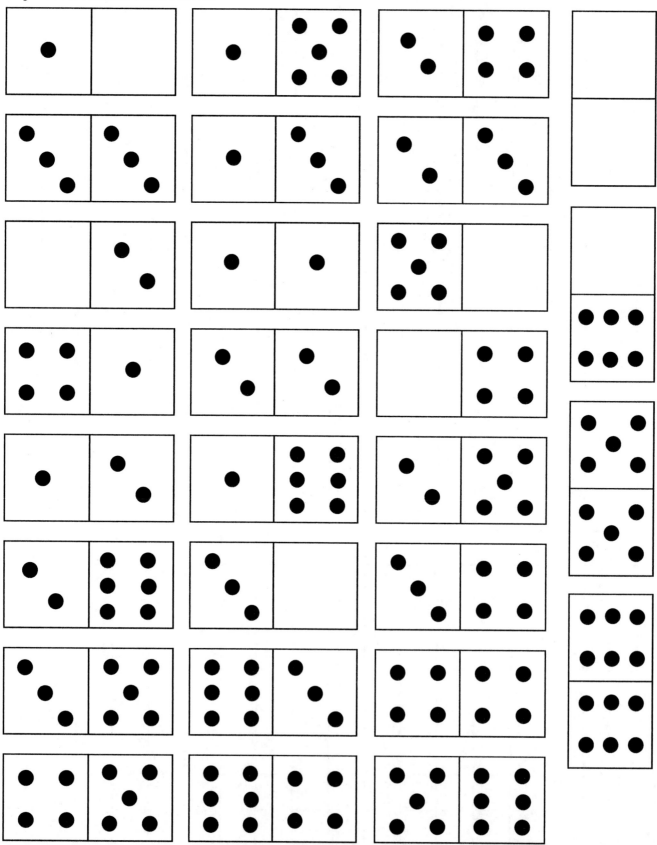

Recording Geoboard Designs

Reproduce, laminate, and cut out.

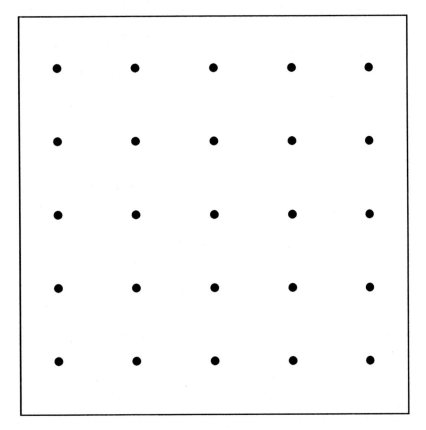

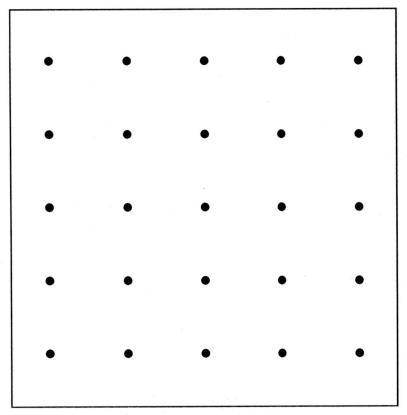

Equivalents Chart

Length

Standard
1 foot (ft.) = 12 inches (in.)
1 yard (yd.) = 3 feet (ft.)
1 yard (yd.) = 36 inches (in.)
1 mile (mi.) = 5280 feet (ft.)
1 mile (mi.) = 1760 yards (yd.)

Metric
1 centimeter (cm) = 10 millimeters (mm)
1 meter (m) = 100 centimeters (cm)
1 kilometer (km) = 1000 meters (m)

Weight

Standard
1 pound (lb.) = 16 ounces (oz.)
1 ton (T) = 2000 pounds (lb.)

Metric
1 gram (gm) = 1000 milligrams (mg)
1 kilogram (kg) = 1000 grams (gm)

Area

Standard
1 square foot (ft.) = 144 square inches (sq. in.)
1 square yard (yd.) = 9 square feet (sq. ft.)

Metric
1 square meter (m) = 10,000 square cm (sq. cm)
1 hectare (ha) = 10,000 square meters (sq. m)

Capacity

Standard
1 tablespoon (T) = 3 teaspoons (t.)
1 cup (c.) = 8 fluid ounces (fl. oz.)
1 pint (pt.) = 2 cups (c.)
1 quart (qt.) = 2 pints (pt.)
1 gallon (gal.) = 4 quarts (qt.)

Metric
1 teaspoon (t.) = 5 milliliters (mL)
1 tablespoon (T) = 12.5 milliliters (mL)
1 liter (L) = 1000 milliliters (mL)
1 kilometer (kL) = 1000 liters (L)

Temperature

Fahrenheit
212° F boiling point of water
32° F   freezing point of water
98.6° F body temperature

Celsius
100° C boiling point of water
0° C   freezing point of water
37° C   body temperature

Math Center Model

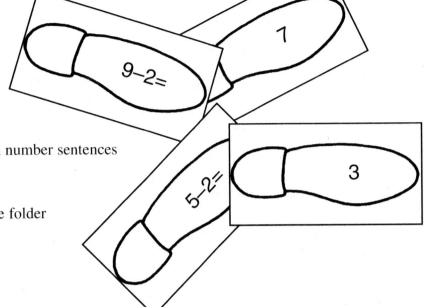

Activity:

Cover Your Tracks

Skill:

Subtracting basic facts to 9

Objective:

To match answers with subtraction number sentences

Materials:

- poster board, tagboard, or file folder
- string-tie envelope
- glue or rubber cement
- markers or colored pencils
- scissors

Directions:

1. Reproduce pages 168–170 and glue them to poster board, tagboard, or a file folder.

2. Cut out the answer footprints on page 169 and put them in a string-tie envelope with the answer key.

3. Attach a string-tie envelope to the back of the center with rubber cement.

Additional Activities:

1. Have students make self-checking study cards. Students will need poster board, scissors, markers, and a hole punch.

   a.   Have students trace the outline of their own feet (with shoes on) and cut them out.

   b.   Have students write the number sentences for subtraction facts: 0–5 on one and 6–9 on the other.

   c.   Instead of writing the answer after the equal sign, have students punch a hole in the card and stick a pencil through the hole.

   d.   Have students turn the footprint card over and write the correct answer to the number sentence next to the hole with the pencil poked through it.

   e.   Students can use the cards to practice subtraction facts by themselves or with a partner and can poke-through to check their answers.

2. Using the same format as Cover Your Tracks, create activities to reinforce basic subtraction facts to 18 and basic addition facts to sums of 9 and 18.

Cover Your Tracks (cont.)

Hide the subtraction facts by covering the tracks.

Directions:

1. Take the cards out of the envelope.

2. Complete the number sentence in each footprint and find the card with the answer. Cover the footprint with the card.

3. When you have finished covering all the footprints, use the answer key to check your work.

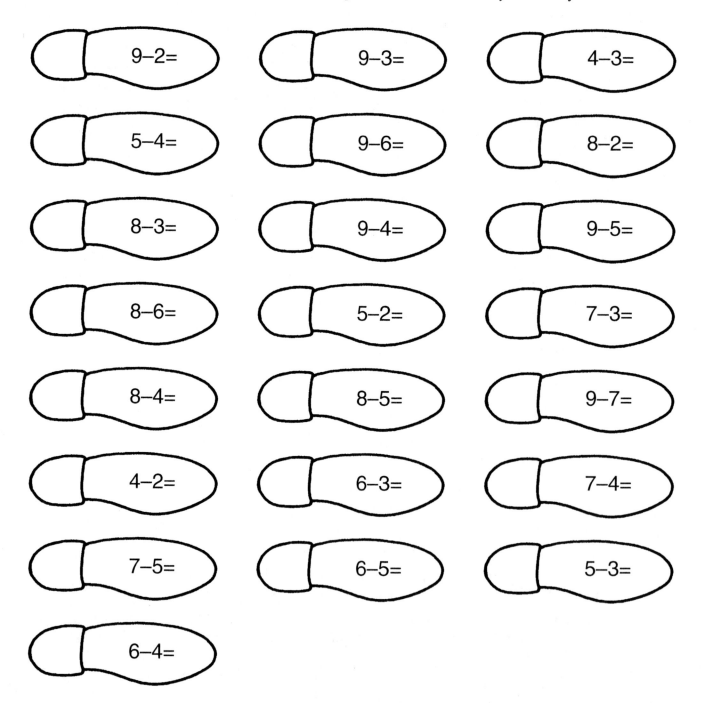

Cover Your Tracks (cont.)
—Answer Footprints

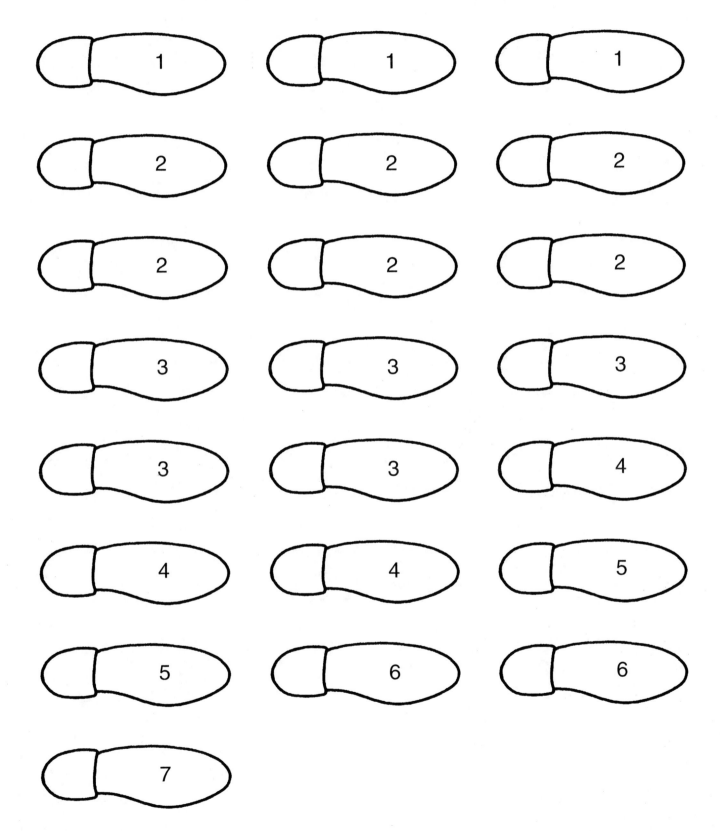

Cover Your Tracks (cont.) —Answer Key

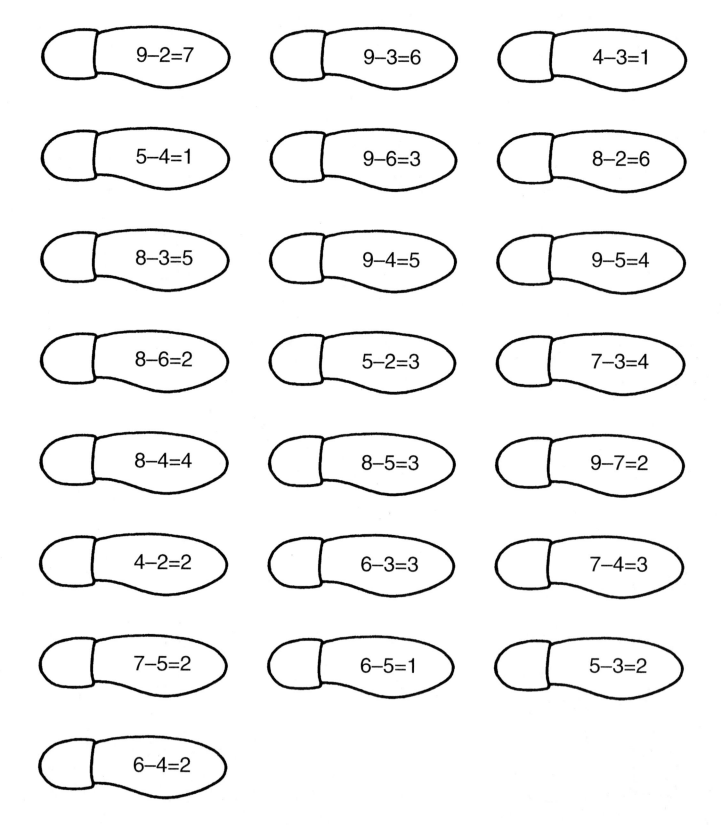

9–2=7

9–3=6

4–3=1

5–4=1

9–6=3

8–2=6

8–3=5

9–4=5

9–5=4

8–6=2

5–2=3

7–3=4

8–4=4

8–5=3

9–7=2

4–2=2

6–3=3

7–4=3

7–5=2

6–5=1

5–3=2

6–4=2

Science Centers

Science Centers *(cont.)*

Science centers provide students with valuable hands-on opportunities that help them relate science to the world around them. The materials listed for the suggested types of displays and experiments should be augmented by two crucial pieces of equipment—a hand lens (magnifying glass) and a specimen box (bug box) with a magnifying lid.

Aquatic Life

- large aquarium
- small plastic containers for minnows, goldfish, or tadpoles
- materials for float-and-sink experiments
- dishpans
- measuring cups and spoons
- plastic bottles and empty containers of different sizes and shapes
- plastic lids
- waterproof aprons
- small plastic boats; boats made by teacher or students
- seashell collections—one for display only and another for sorting, measuring, counting, etc.
- water fun collection—tubes, funnels, bits of wood, etc.
- bubble-making materials
- doll clothes and plastic dishes to wash
- clothesline

Plant Life

- different soil samples, such as sand and potting soil
- plastic bags
- plastic flower pots and other containers, such as egg cartons, milk cartons, and butter tubs
- variety of plant seeds
- small tools for indoor gardening
- large trays and watering can
- desert garden
- terrarium
- gloves
- string
- assortment of plants and plant parts, such as pine cones, avocado pits, driftwood, bark, tree limbs, twigs, acorns, weeds, cattails, leaves, etc.

Science Centers (cont.)

Magnetism

- various shapes and sizes of magnets
- assortment of magnetic objects, such as coins, iron filings, paper clips, etc.
- small clear plastic containers
- magnet kits, such as Magnet Discovery Board (manufactured by Lakeshore)
- magnet games and activities, such as Magna Doodle (manufactured by Ideal)

Life Science

- posters or flannel board pieces of body parts
- antlers and horns
- feathers
- eggshells
- insect and spider collections
- insect nests
- honeycomb
- bird's nest (keep in plastic bag)
- snake skin
- turtle shell
- animal teeth
- seashells
- classroom pets—earthworms, birds, hamsters, tadpoles, fish, etc.
- farm and zoo toys or models
- microscopes and slides

Process Skills

- balance scales
- plastic or wood materials and shapes for sorting
- animal camouflage cards
- kaleidoscope
- color paddles
- thermometers
- prisms
- calendars and clocks
- mirrors
- audiotaped animal sounds
- musical instruments
- giant magnifier

Earth and Space Science

- fossils, petrified wood, and amber
- rock collection
- common rock – chalk, salt, flint, etc.
- pictures of the four seasons
- toy dinosaurs
- space toys
- model of the solar system
- globe
- world map

Science Observation Journals

Have students make and regularly use a science journal to record their observations, predictions, and conclusions as they work alone, in pairs, or in groups in the Science Center. Model for the class how to observe and record changes they see in their science explorations. By asking probing questions rather than explaining, lead class discussions about predicting and drawing conclusions as changes occur.

How To Make a Science Observation Journal

1. Reproduce a copy of page 175 and five copies of page 176 for each journal.

2. Use construction paper for a cover.

3. Insert the journal pages inside the cover pages and staple them together along the top or left edge.

4. Cover the stapled edge with tape.

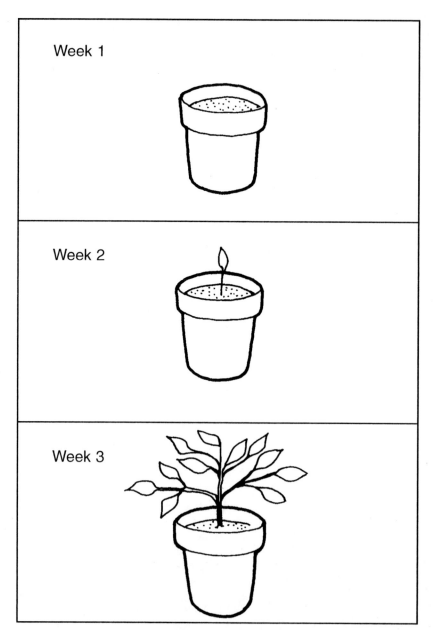

Week 1

Week 2

Week 3

Science Observation Journal

Name _____

Date	What I Observed	What I Think Will Happen Next

Science Observation
Journal *(cont.)*

Name _____ Date _____

Draw the changes you observed.

This is what happened. _____

_____

_____

_____

_____

This is what I learned. _____

_____

_____

_____

_____

Science Center Model

Activity:

Uncovering Dirt

Skill:

To learn about soils

Objective:

To understand differences among soil types

Materials:

- about 3 cups (705 mL) each of an assortment of soils, such as sand, garden soil, potting soil, etc.
- a container with a lid for each type of soil sample
- toothpicks
- magnifying glass
- large pieces of scrap paper
- trash can

Directions:

1. Reproduce pages 178 and 179 for students.
2. Label the soil samples with letters so students can keep track.
3. Place the worksheet pages and the other materials in the Science Center.
4. Model for students how to use the soil and the worksheets.
5. Lead a discussion about soils and their suitability for different purposes.

Additional Activities:

1. Get several sizes of gravel and sand to show how rocks get progressively smaller until they are dirt. Discuss how different types of erosion help create dirt.
2. Have students look for examples of erosion on the school grounds.

Science Center Model *(cont.)*

Lab Worksheet—A

Ask Yourself

What is dirt made of?

_____ 1 sample of dirt

_____ 1 toothpick

_____ 1 magnifying glass

_____ 1 piece of paper

What You Do

_____ 1. Put your dirt on the paper.

_____ 2. Look at it through the magnifying glass.

_____ 3. Use a toothpick to spread it around.

_____ 3. Count how many different types of things you see in the dirt. You may see rocks, bits of plants or twigs, or even an insect or animal.

_____ 5. When you are finished, throw away your dirt sample.

What You Learned

How many different types of things were in the dirt? _____

Science Center Model *(cont.)*

Lab Worksheet—B

Ask Yourself

What is dirt made of?

What You Need

_____ 2 samples of dirt, A and B

_____ 1 magnifying glass

_____ 1 toothpick

_____ 1 piece of paper

What You Do

_____ 1. Put a small amount of dirt from Sample A on the paper.

_____ 2. Look at it through the magnifying glass. Use the toothpick to spread it around.

_____ 3. On the chart below, write down the number of rocks, plant parts, and animal parts you find.

_____ 4. Throw away your dirt from Sample A.

_____ 5. Now place a small amount of dirt from Sample B on the paper.

_____ 6. Repeat Steps 2–4 for Sample B.

	How Many?		
	Rocks	Plant Parts	Animals
Dirt Sample A			
Dirt Sample B			

What You Learned

Dirt is mostly made of _____

How are the two types of dirt different? _____

_____

Social Studies Centers

The Importance of Social Studies

Social studies and geography instruction are gaining importance in the primary grades. Learning to appreciate other cultures is a high priority as America continues to become more ethnically diverse and the economy becomes ever more global.

Students must begin early to gain an understanding of the world they live in. Make having a current globe and updated maps in your classroom a priority and refer to them often.

Use the self-evaluation forms on pages 187–188 to put into Social Studies Centers for students to use as they explore our world through activities and reading. Below are suggested materials for including in a Social Studies Center.

Materials:

- tape recorder
- tapes of songs from around the world
- foreign language tapes
- materials for making envelopes and stamps
- stamps from around the world
- flags from different countries
- social studies kits and games
- poster of children from other lands
- posters or objects from other countries
- postcards
- newspapers and magazines
- maps and globes
- map puzzles
- toy telephones
- outlines of continents, countries, states
- books about countries and people around the world

The World

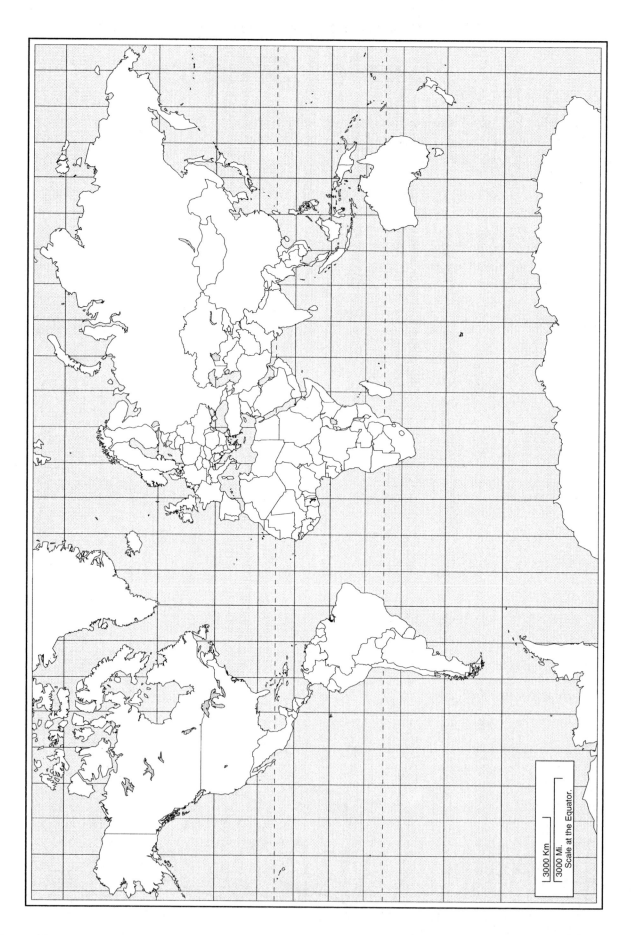

3000 Km
3000 Mi.
Scale at the Equator.

North America

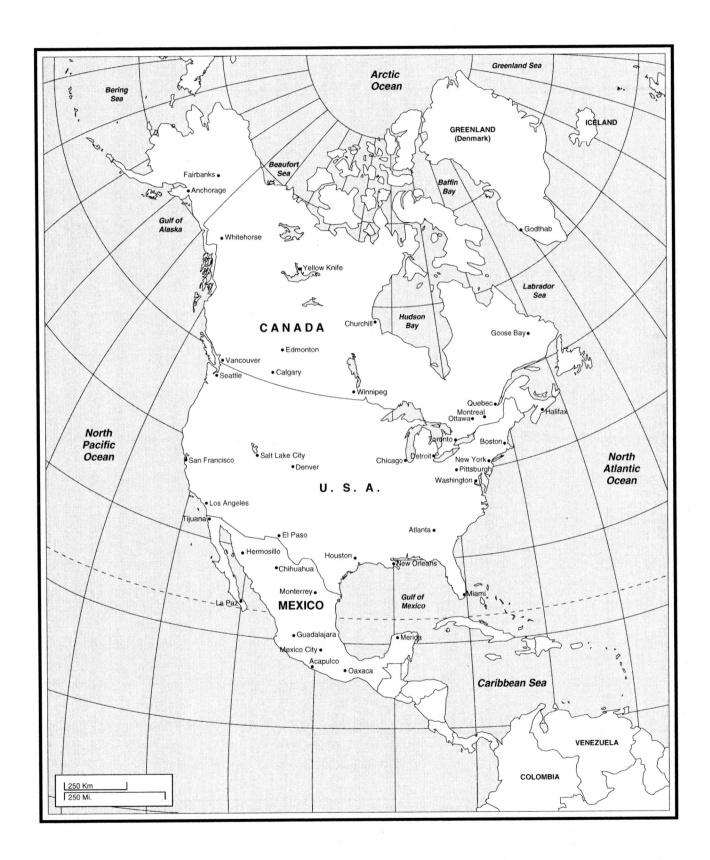

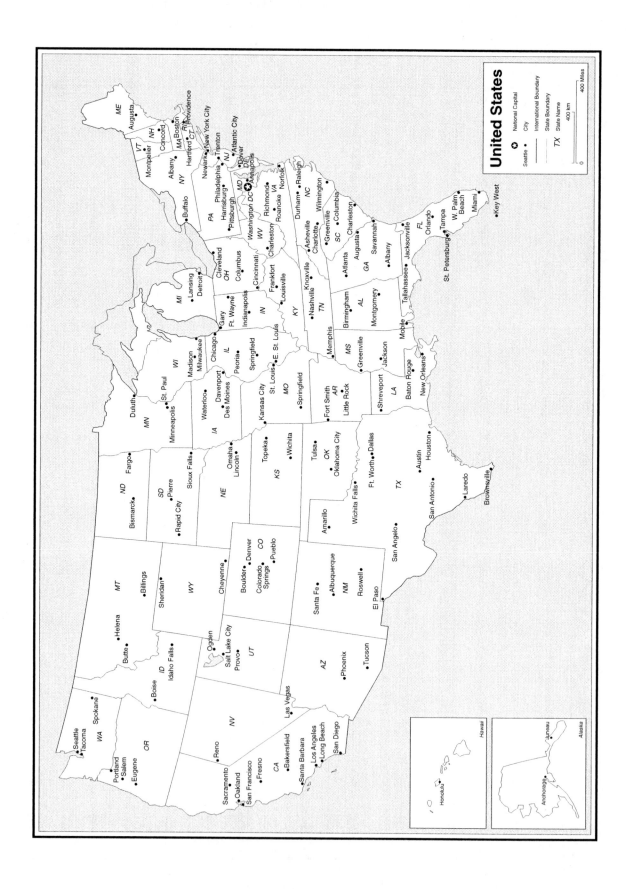

Canada

Canada

- National Capital
- Calgary • City
- International Boundary
- Provincial Boundary
- *Quebec* Province Name

500 km

0 — 500 Miles

Map labels:
- Dawson
- Yukon Territory
- Whitehorse
- *Great Bear Lake*
- Victoria Island
- Baffin Island
- Northwest Territories
- *Great Slave Lake*
- Yellowknife
- British Columbia
- Alberta
- *Lake Athabasca*
- Edmonton
- Saskatchewan
- Manitoba
- Churchill
- Newfoundland
- Victoria • Vancouver
- Calgary
- Saskatoon
- St. John's
- Regina
- *Lake Winnipeg*
- Quebec
- Winnipeg
- Ontario
- P.E.I.
- Sydney
- New Brunswick
- Fredericton
- Halifax
- Nova Scotia
- Thunder Bay
- *Lake Superior*
- Quebec
- Montreal
- *Lake Huron*
- Ottawa
- *Lake Michigan*
- Toronto
- *Lake Ontario*
- *Lake Erie*

States/Provinces and Capitals

United States

State	Capital	State	Capital
Alabama	Montgomery	Montana	Helena
Alaska	Juneau	Nebraska	Lincoln
Arizona	Phoenix	Nevada	Carson City
Arkansas	Little Rock	New Hampshire	Concord
California	Sacramento	New Jersey	Trenton
Colorado	Denver	New Mexico	Santa Fe
Connecticut	Hartford	New York	Albany
Delaware	Dover	North Carolina	Raleigh
Florida	Tallahassee	North Dakota	Bismarck
Georgia	Atlanta	Ohio	Columbus
Hawaii	Honolulu	Oklahoma	Oklahoma City
Idaho	Boise	Oregon	Salem
Illinois	Springfield	Pennsylvania	Harrisburg
Indiana	Indianapolis	Rhode Island	Providence
Iowa	Des Moines	South Carolina	Columbia
Kansas	Topeka	South Dakota	Pierre
Kentucky	Frankfort	Tennessee	Nashville
Louisiana	Baton Rouge	Texas	Austin
Maine	Augusta	Utah	Salt Lake City
Maryland	Annapolis	Vermont	Montpelier
Massachusetts	Boston	Virginia	Richmond
Michigan	Lansing	Washington	Olympia
Minnesota	St. Paul	West Virginia	Charleston
Mississippi	Jackson	Wisconsin	Madison
Missouri	Jefferson City	Wyoming	Cheyenne

Canada

Province/Territory	Capital
Alberta	Edmonton
British Columbia	Victoria
Manitoba	Winnipeg
New Brunswick	Fredericton
Newfoundland	St. John's
Northwest Territories	Yellowknife
Nova Scotia	Halifax
Ontario	Toronto
Prince Edward Island	Charlottetown
Quebec	Quebec
Saskatchewan	Regina
Yukon	Whitehorse

Social Studies Concepts Self-Evaluation—Grades K-2

Write or draw in the top boxes before doing your activity. Write or draw in the bottom box after you complete your activity.

Name _____ Date _____

Topic:_____

What I know.	What I want to know.

What I learned.

Social Studies Concepts Self-Evaluation—Grades 3-6

Name _____ Date _____

Topic of Study _____

What do you already know about the topic? (Answer this before your activity.)

What did you learn about the topic? (Answer this after your activity.)

What else do you need to know about the topic?

Social Studies Center Model

Reproduce and cut apart the country cards on pages 189 and 190. Place them in a box at the Social Studies Center. Have each student draw a card and research that country's flag. Provide materials for the students to draw and color the flags. Display the completed flags in a border around the room.

Afghanistan	Albania	Algeria	Argentina	Australia
Austria	Belarus	Belgium	Botswana	Brazil
Cambodia	Canada	Chad	Chile	China
Colombia	Costa Rica	Czech Republic	Denmark	Ecuador
England	Egypt	El Salvador	Estonia	Ethiopia
France	Germany	Greece	Guam	Guatemala

Social Studies Center Model (cont.)

Honduras	Hungary	India	Iran	Iraq
Italy	Japan	Liberia	Jordan	Mexico
Morocco	Netherlands	New Zealand	Nigeria	Pakistan
Panama	Russia	Saudi Arabia	Scotland	Slovakia
South Africa	Spain	Sweden	Switzerland	Syria
Thailand	Turkey	United States	Venezuela	Zaire

Research Centers

Research Centers *(cont.)*

Thanks to CD–ROM technology, every classroom that has a computer can also have an encyclopedia. Locate your Research Center near the Computer Center. Provide an assortment of dictionaries, including picture dictionaries. The school library will probably have a variety of easy dictionaries. Bring several types to the classroom to review. Then have students try them out. Different dictionaries can vary greatly in quality, and you will want to be very discriminating as to which ones you buy or check out for your classroom. Make students aware of the importance of finding and using the most current information possible when doing research.

As a new research theme is introduced, you will notice that students show more interest in some books than in others. Popular books can stay in the Research Center even after the thematic unit is completed. You may wish to place a removable colored coding dot on the books' spines and place them together. On your list of thematic materials, place a star beside the books that prompted sustained student interest. If you have funds allocated for your classroom, you may wish to use the money to make these books permanent additions to your library. Ask for parent volunteers to produce audiotapes to go along with the texts of favorite books.

Suggested Reading

Eyewitness Books Series by Alfred A. Knopf

New True Books Series by Childrens Press

Ranger Rick is an outstanding magazine for primary children. It has great nature photos, and it is all about animals and natural history. (ages 6–12)

Zoobooks is a series of books. They have animal facts with terrific photos and art. Each issue is about one subject, such as dolphins or elephants. (ages 7–14)

Kids Discover is as science-oriented magazine. It also focuses on just one subject, such as volcanoes or weather, in each issue. (ages 6–12)

Kid City is about sports and interesting kids. (ages 6–10)

Disney Adventures features the Disney characters. There are informational articles about travel, music, and Disney movies and entertainment. (ages 6–14)

Spider is a magazine of stories, comics, and puzzles. (ages 6–9)

Crayola Kids (ages 3–8) or *Pack-O-Fun* (ages 6–12) can be used to give students ideas for projects.

Family PC may be of as much interest to you as it is to students. There are a variety of stimulating ideas to use on the classroom computer, including computer crafts. This may be the intellectual challenge you are looking for. (ages 6–adult)

Go to the library for some back copies of these magazines: *Your Big Backyard, Chickadee, Ladybug,* and *Sesame Street.* They are recommended for younger children but also provide independent reading for reluctant readers.

You may wish to ask parents to donate discarded magazines that would be appropriate for students to use in the classroom.

Research Center Model

Activity:

Endangered Species

Skills:

Using a variety of research materials and techniques to learn more about a topic

Using researched material to prepare a report and an oral presentation

Objective:

To build awareness of global environmental issues through investigation of endangered species

Materials:

- 3 pieces of poster board
- 3 envelopes 9" x 12" (23 cm x 30 cm)
- books and magazines about endangered animal species
- sample animal mask
- Endangered Species Chart (page 195)
- Animal Interview Picture (page 196)
- 1 #10 envelope for each student
- 1 large grocery bag per student
- 10 lined index cards 3" x 5" (8 cm x 13 cm) per student
- 1 Note Cards worksheet (page 197) per student
- at least 1 Bibliography Cards page (page 198) per student
- 1 set of Animal Interview worksheets (pages 199–202) per student
- 1 World Map (page 182) per student
- crayons or markers
- paper scraps

Directions:

1. Prepare the center. A suggested layout is on page 32.
2. Introduce the center to the class. Have students decide on the animal they wish to study.
3. Distribute index cards, an envelope, and a Note Cards worksheet to each student. Explain how to prepare and use the note cards.
4. Distribute a Bibliography Cards page to each student and model how to create a bibliography. (Put extra sheets in an envelope in the center.) Allow time for students to read and record data. This can be done during reading time, assigned as homework, or both.
5. Distribute a set of Animal Interview worksheets to each student. Model the activity, and allow time for students to complete it in class or assign it as homework. Call students' attention to the sample folder and mask in the research center display.
6. Have students give oral presentations to the class. Photographs of the interviews make a fun and interesting display.

Note: Allow six to ten working periods of 30–45 minutes (class time or as homework) for completion of all the activities.

Endangered Species

Endangered Species Chart

Reproduce the chart, cut it out, and mount it on heavy paper. Use a brad to attach the wheel to the research center display.

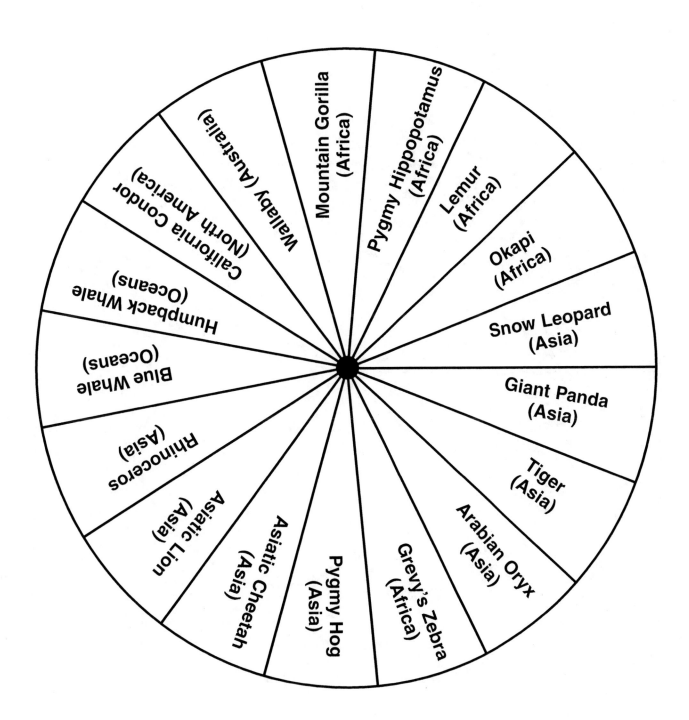

Animal Interview Picture

Reproduce the picture onto heavy paper. Color it, cut it out, and attach it to the research center display.

Writing a Research Report: Note Cards

1. The first step in writing a research report is deciding what you want to learn about. Select one of the endangered animals from the wheel.

   I have decided to learn about _____.

2. The next step is to read about your animal and take notes. Do not copy word for word from the book. This is stealing someone else's work. It is called plagiarism.

Note Cards:

1. Cut out the topic boxes below and glue each one across the top of an index card.

2. When you read a fact on that topic, write it on the card.

3. Keep all the cards in an envelope so you don't lose them.

What it eats (Food)

Animal's name and description	**What it eats (Food)**
How it raises its young	**What are its enemies**
Other interesting facts	**Where it lives (Habitat)**
How it reproduces	**Why it is endangered**
How it protects itself	**Other interesting facts**

Writing a Research Report: Bibliography Cards

- You must keep track of the books and magazines you read and take information from. This is called making a bibliography, and it lets people know where you got your information.

- When you write facts on your note cards, also write down the information about the book or magazine the facts came from. Be sure to record this information before you take the book back to the library.

- A good research project uses more than one source.

Book

_____ | _____
author's last name | author's first name

_____
name of book (underlined)

_____
publisher

_____, _____
page numbers   copyright date

Magazine

_____ | _____
author's last name | author's first name

" _____ "
name of article (in quotation marks)

_____
name of magazine (underlined)

_____, _____
page numbers   issue month and year

Teacher Note: Reproduce these on heavy paper so students may cut them apart and store them with their note cards. Place extras in the research center for students' use.

Writing a Research Report: Animal Interview

Your research notes are finished. You have learned a great deal about your animal. Now pretend you are a reporter and that your endangered animal can talk. Using your Note Cards, prepare an interview for Animals Talk Back, a television show about endangered species.

1. Use pages 199–200 to plan and record your interview.
2. Use page 201 for Putting It All Together in a research report folder.
3. Use page 202 to prepare an oral presentation of your interview.

Animals Talk Back

An interview with a (an)_____

(your animal)

by reporter_____

(your name)

I'm here in _____

(continent)

with an endangered species. Could you please describe yourself for our viewers?_____

_____

_____

Tell us about your habitat. _____

_____

_____

What are your favorite foods? _____

_____

_____

How are your young born?_____

_____

_____

Writing a Research Report: Animal Interview *(cont.)*

How do you care for your young? _____

_____

_____

_____

Who are your natural enemies? _____

_____

_____

_____

How can you protect yourself?_____

_____

_____

_____

I know you are an endangered species. What are the main reasons for this?

_____

_____

_____

_____

We have a worldwide audience. Millions of people are watching and listening. What would you like to tell them to help them understand you and your situation?

_____

_____

_____

_____

_____

Writing a Research Report: Putting It All Together

1. Get or make a folder for your report. On the front put the title, your name, and the date.

2. Make a title page. This is the same as the folder cover but it's really the first page of your report.

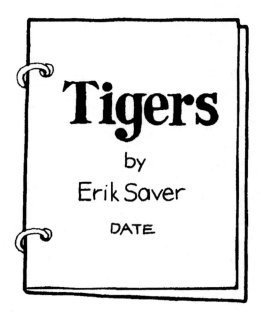

3. Next put in your Animal Interview pages. Be sure someone has checked them for neatness and spelling. Recopy them if necessary.

4. Then add a map to show where your animal lives. Get a world map from the Research Center. Label the continent(s) and color the part where your animal lives.

5. Draw and label several pictures of your animal doing what it does. Put them behind the map.

6. Finally, use your Bibliography Cards to create a written bibliography. Check the sample folder in the Research Center display to make sure you put it in the correct form.

7. Make sure all your pages are in order, and finish the folder by stapling or binding. Decorate your report cover.

Research Report Oral Presentation

1. Make a mask of your animal. See the Research Center display for a sample and the things you will need.

2. Read and reread your report until you really know the answers to all the questions. Wear your mask for the interview.

3. Have a partner be the reporter and ask you the interview questions from your report.

4. Speak slowly, clearly, and loudly.

5. Put yourself in the place of your animal and use all your power to inform and influence your audience.

6. Have fun!

Computer Centers

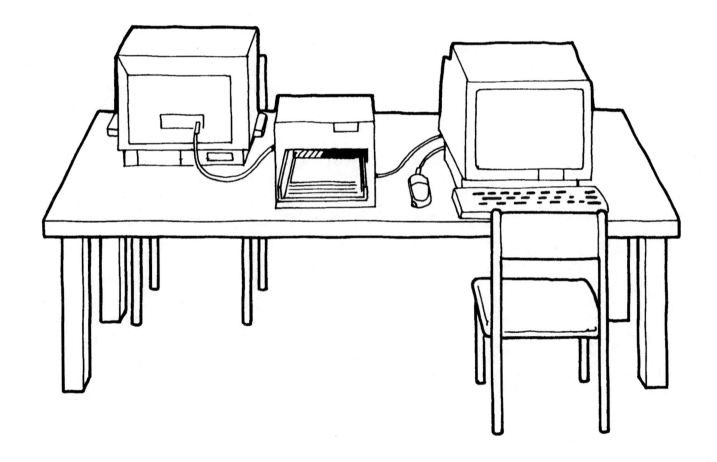

Computer Centers *(cont.)*

Computer Comfort

Students should become familiar with and comfortable using computers as soon as possible. To do this, they need to know:

- Basic computer vocabulary—computer, hardware, keyboard, mouse, monitor, screen, hard drive, disk drive, printer, diskette, CD–ROM, software, program, cursor, space bar, enter/return, arrow keys, insert, delete, open, save, and print

- How to use and care for computer hardware

- How to use computer software—mainly programing and word processing

Word Processing

As with all skills, some students will be ready to learn how to type before others. Therefore, primary students must be allowed to progress at their own rates.

Allowing students to use a word processing program on the computer is extremely important because they can reinforce their reading and writing skills while learning a skill crucial to success in a technological era.

Word processing instruction can begin at the kindergarten level. Even very young children easily learn word processing when given appropriate instruction and access to computers, and composing on them may even be easier than using a pencil and paper. Using a computer can help decrease a student's fear of failure or feelings of boredom since text can be revised without having to rewrite the entire work.

CD–ROMs and Diskettes

Most new computers use CD-ROMs in addition to diskettes. CD-ROMs can store an enormous amount of information. For example, an entire encyclopedia can be stored on just one CD. Computers with CD-ROMs have full-motion video capabilities with sound and text. Many also offer a range of multimedia capabilities that allow users to create their own productions. Eventually most computers used in schools will have CD-ROM capabilities. However, because of the cost involved, it may take school districts time to update or replace the computers and software they are currently using. Be sure to match your school's hardware with your class's software needs.

Suggested Software

Suggested Software

MECC

6160 Summit Drive North

Minneapolis, Minnesota 55430-4003

Title	System Requirements	Level
Counting Critters	Apple 64K	PreK–K
First-Letter Fun	Apple 64K	PreK–K
Sum Stories	Apple 128K	K–2
Paint with Words	Apple 64K	PreK–2
Storybook Weaver Deluxe	CD-ROM for MAC and Windows	1–6
USA Geography	MAC; CD-ROM for MAC	1–7

Broderbund

P.O. Box 6125

Novato, California 94948-6125

Phone: 1-800-457-4509

Title	System Requirements	Level	Other Information
Living Books • Little Monster at School • Harry and the Haunted House • Arthur's Birthday • Arthur's Teacher Trouble • The Tortoise and the Hare • other titles available	CD-ROM for MAC and Multimedia PC	Ages 3-8 Ages 3-8 Ages 6-10 Ages 6-10 Ages 3-8	Interactive screens; full-motion animation scenes; storybooks; games; teaching guides; songs
Math Workshop	CD-ROM for MAC and Windows	Ages 6-12	
Where in the World Is Carmen Sandiego? Junior Detective Edition	CD-ROM for MAC and Multimedia PC	Ages 4-8	Features clues and problem solving; requires no reading

The Learning Company

545 Middlefield Road

Menlo Park, California 94025

Title	System Requirements	Level
Reader Rabbit 1	MAC; CD-ROM for MAC and Windows	K–1
Reader Rabbit 2	MAC; CD-ROM for MAC and Windows	1–3

Suggested Software (cont.)

National Geographic Educational Services
P.O. Box 98018
Washington, D.C. 20090-8018
Phone: 1-800-368-2728

Title	System Requirements	Level	Other Information
National Geographic's Wonders of Learning • Various titles available	CD-ROM for MAC and Windows	Primary	Narrated texts; music; special ESL feature

IBM (K–12 Education)
Call for catalogues, product information, and location of the nearest dealer: 1-800-426-4338

Title	System Requirements	Level	Other Information
Write Along	Audio units; Printer; IBM or Compatible; Network and stand-alone versions available on disks and CD-ROM	K–2	Word processing; graphics; text-to-speech audio feedback for editing; draw editor for illustrations
Writing to Read 2000	IBM or Compatible; Network and stand-alone versions available on disks and CD-ROM	K–1	Features clues and problem solving; requires no reading

Sunburst
101 Castleton Street
Pleasantville, New York 10570-0100
Phone: 1-800-321-7511

Title	System Requirements	Level	Other Information
Muppet Slate	Apple II (128 K); graphics printer recommended	K–3	Word and picture processing program
Number Connections	MAC (2 MB)	K–3	Real problem solving; emphasizes process; has a word-processor
Balancing Bear	MAC, Apple II, IBM or Compatible, Tandy 100	K–3	Real-life and imaginary problems
Hop to It!	MAC, Apple II	K–3	Number lines; multiple solutions
A to Zap	CD-ROM for MAC or Windows	K–3	Letters, numbers, words
The Pond	MAC, Apple II, IBM or Compatible	K–3	Identifying and describing patterns

Computer Match-Up

Matching: Draw a line from each of the words to a picture that means the same thing.

keyboard

monitor

CD-ROM

floppy disk

disk drive

mouse

mouse pad

CD

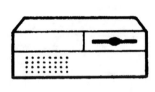

Write each of the words here. Use a space or a comma between each word.

_____

_____

_____

_____

_____

_____

_____

Art Centers

Art Centers *(cont.)*

Integrating art with reading, writing, listening, and speaking is a wonderful way to get students motivated and engaged actively in learning. Analyzing characteristics and details in order to draw requires high-level thinking skills and refined hand-eye coordination. When children use the Art Center, encourage them to also write words to label or sentences to describe their creations. Suggested basic supplies include:

- crayons
- washable markers
- colored pencils
- scissors
- easels
- glue sticks
- construction paper
- white art paper
- newsprint
- liquid tempera paints

- variety of paintbrushes
- white liquid glue
- water containers/sink
- watercolor paints
- pastel chalk
- rulers
- shapes to trace
- photographs of items pertaining to your theme
- step-by-step instruction books
- stencils (letters and pictures)

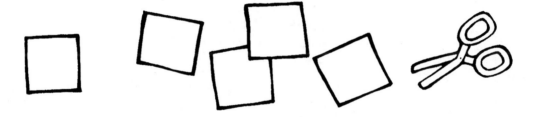

Edible Play Clay

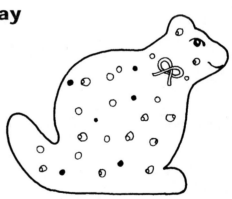

Materials:

- 1 cup (250 mL) peanut butter
- 1 cup (250 mL) light corn syrup
- 1 1/4 cups (300 mL) sifted (10x) sugar
- 1 1/2 cups (375 mL) powdered milk
- bowl

Directions:

1. Combine all the ingredients in a bowl and knead well.
2. Have students wash their hands, then give them each a ball of dough.
3. Provide edible items such as chocolate chips, pretzel sticks, or jelly beans for students to use to create sculptures.
4. When students are finished, have them show their sculpture to the class.
5. Let students eat their sculptures.

Inedible Play Clay

Flour Clay

Materials:

- 2 cups (500 mL) flour
- 1 cup (250 mL) water
- 1 cup (250 mL) salt
- 2 tablespoon (30 mL) alum
- 2 tablespoons (30 mL) cooking oil
- various colors of liquid food coloring
- bowl

Directions:

1. Knead all the ingredients together in a bowl until the mixture is smooth and pliable.

2. Knead in the food coloring. (Wear rubber gloves to prevent staining your hands.)

Salt Clay
(for baked clay creations)

Materials:

- 2 cups (500 mL) flour
- $^1/_2$ cup (125 mL) salt
- 2 tablespoons (30 mL) cooking oil
- $^1/_2$ cup–$^3/_4$ cup (125 mL–180 mL) water
- food coloring
- bowl
- cookie sheet
- oven

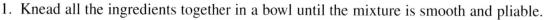

Directions:

1. Mix together the flour, salt, and oil in a bowl.

2. Add $^1/_2$ cup (125 mL) of water and knead. Add more water as necessary to make the dough smooth and pliable.

3. Knead in the food coloring. Wear rubber gloves to prevent staining your hands.

4. To bake, place the formed objects on a cookie sheet. Bake them at 350° F (177° C) until they are golden brown and firm to a gentle touch.

Art Center Model

The art of quilling, sometimes called paper filigree, is the technique of creating designs with narrow strips of paper that have been rolled, shaped, arranged, and then affixed onto a background. Historically, the narrow strips were tightly wrapped around the quill of a feather to produce the curled shapes.

Materials:

- cardboard covered with wax paper
- narrow strips of paper in various colors
- white glue
- straight pins
- pencils
- toothpicks
- basic quilling rolls examples
- sample designs (page 212)

Directions:

1. Prepare a three-dimensional chart of the various quilling rolls and place it in the Art Center for students to see.

2. Demonstrate for the class how to quill.

   a. Moisten the end of a strip of paper and roll it around a pencil.

   b. Carefully slide the paper roll off the pencil and gently bend it into the desired shape.

   c. Make several of each desired shape.

   d. Assemble the rolls using small amounts of glue applied with a toothpick. Work on top of the wax paper and use pins to hold the designs in place while drying.

3. Show students how to glue smaller shapes inside larger ones.

4. When the design has dried, glue it onto a background paper or hang as a mobile.

Basic Quilling Rolls

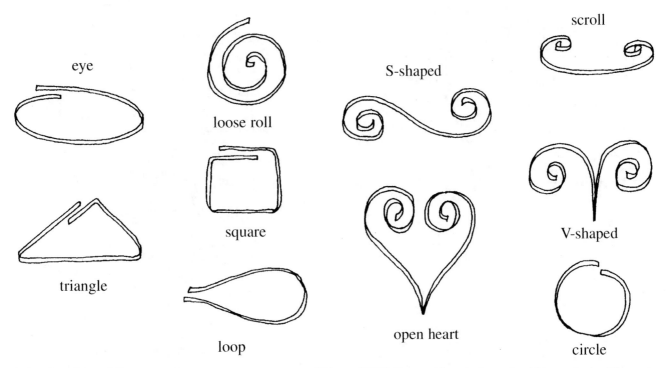

scroll

eye

S-shaped

loose roll

square

V-shaped

triangle

open heart

loop

circle

Sample Quilling Designs

Daisy
7 loops
1 circle
1 scroll

Bird
1 loop
1 V-shaped
3 loose rolls
2 long strips
several circles

Grapes
13 circles
2 loops
1 eye
2 loose rolls

Butterfly
6 circles
1 V-shaped
1 eye
6 loops

Puzzles and Games Centers

Puzzles and games emphasize a variety of skills, among them: sequencing, visual discernment, patterning, fine motor skills, logic, analogies, and creative thinking.

Puzzle Grid—Grades K-2

Use this grid to create word searches and crossword puzzles.

_____   _____

_____   _____

_____   _____

_____   _____

Puzzle Grid—Grades 2-6

Use this grid for word searches and crossword puzzles.

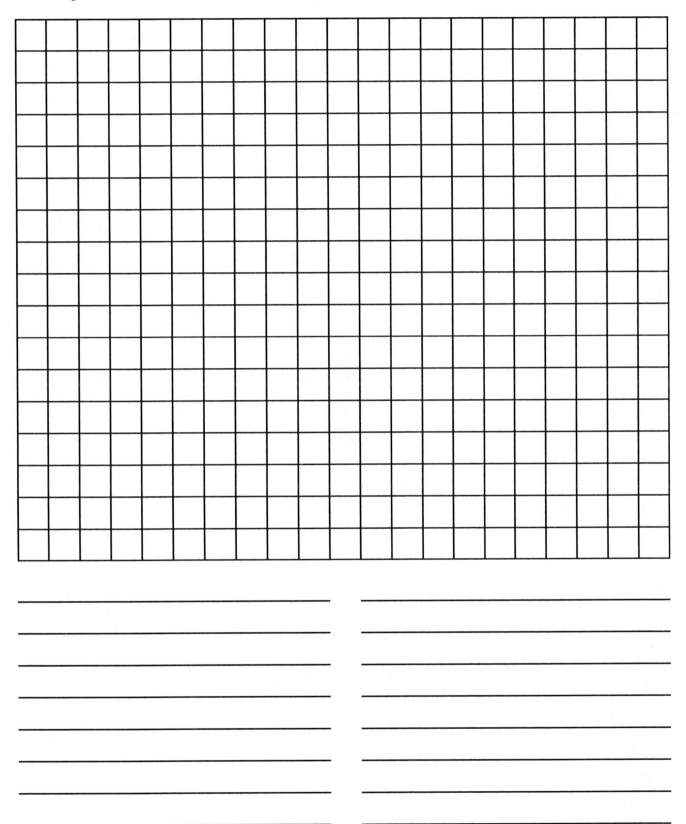

_____   _____

_____   _____

_____   _____

_____   _____

_____   _____

_____   _____

Spinner

Duplicate the wheel and arrow onto sturdy paper. Color the pieces and cut them out. Laminate them. Use a brad to affix the arrow to the wheel so it spins. Use the spinner for games.

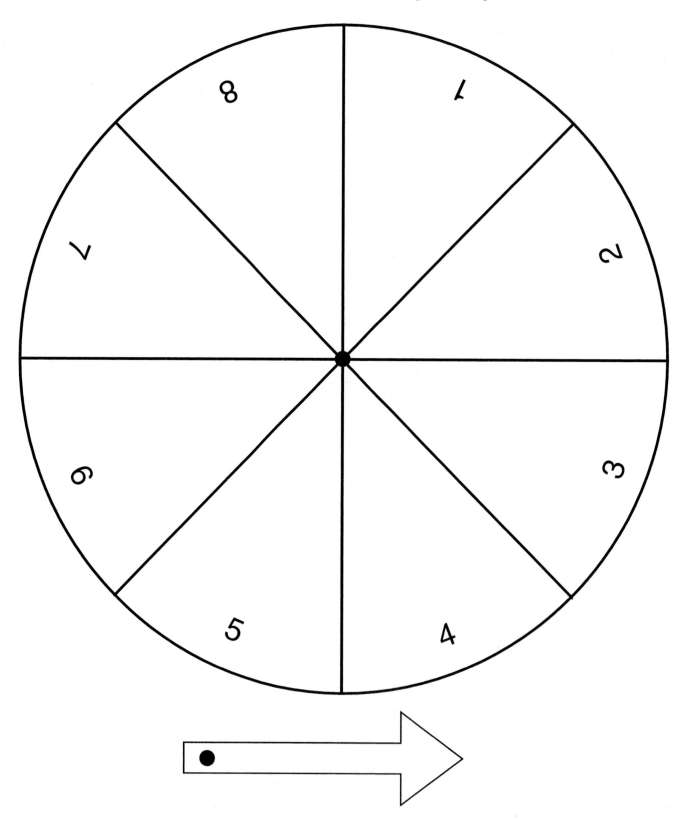

Tumbling Die

Duplicate the pattern onto sturdy paper. Cut out the pattern, fold along the creases, and tape it together.
Use the die for games.

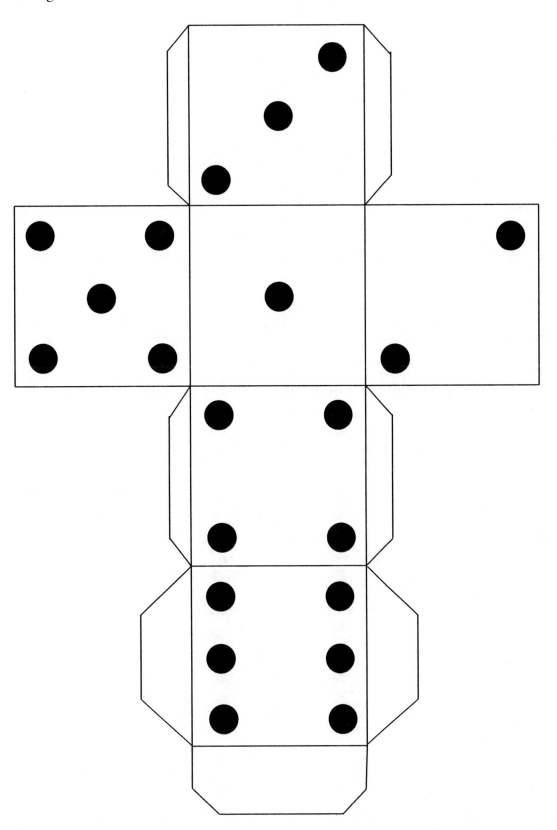

Puzzles and Games Center Model

Activity:

What Comes Next?

Skills:

Sequencing and recognizing patterns

Objective:

To visually determine a pattern and predict the next object in a series

Materials:

- 2 copies of Pattern Puzzles, page 219, colored and laminated
- 1 copy of completed, colored, and laminated Pattern Puzzles page as an answer key
- grease pencil or dry erase marker
- soft cloth for cleaning pattern puzzle

Directions:

1. Place all the materials in the Puzzles and Games Center.
2. Reproduce this page and cut out the sample box below to place in the center.

Other Activities:

1. Provide a collection of real or paper buttons that students can use to create patterns for partners to solve.
2. Use real or paper buttons to create more sequences and glue them to poster board. Have students search and sort the remaining buttons to finish the sequence.

What Comes Next?

Look at each row of buttons. Decide what comes next and draw it in the space.

Example

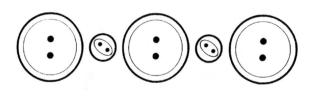

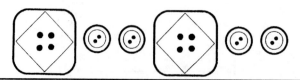

Pattern Puzzles

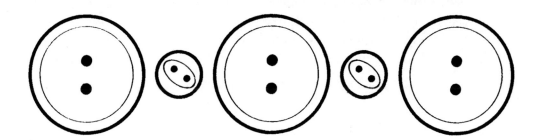

1.

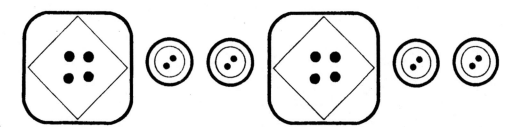

2.

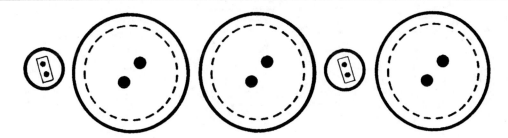

3.

4.

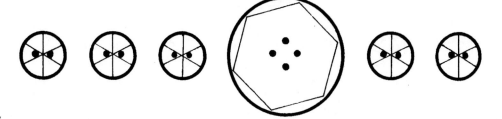

5.

Hands-On Centers

Instead of saying "Don't touch!", this center invites students to handle objects in order to examine them by touch and sight. Encourage students to record what they find in their observation journals (page 174). From time to time, discuss with the class what they have discovered. Change the items frequently. Provide books that will allow students to further research items that interest them.

Recipes for Fun Stuff

Goop

Materials:

- 8 cups (2 L) water
- 1 3/4 cup (400 mL) cornstarch
- 2/3 cup (160 mL) corn syrup
- commercial-size bottles of liquid food coloring (various colors)
- mixing bowls
- resealable plastic bags
- packaging tape
- pan and stove

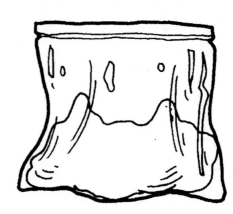

Directions:

1. Combine the first three ingredients in a pan. Cook over medium hear until the goop is thick. Stir occasionally.
2. Let the goop cool slightly. Divide it equally among mixing bowls.
3. Add one color of food coloring to each bowl of goop and stir until the goop is the color you want.
4. Put different quantities of various colors of goop into one baggie and zip the baggie closed. Press out excess air as you close the bag, then seal the opening with packaging tape.
5. Place the bags in the Hands-On Center and allow students to squish and manipulate the goop, watching the colors mix and blend.

Goo

Materials:

- 2 tablespoons (30 mL) water
- 3 tablespoons (45 mL) liquid white glue
- 2 tablespoons (30 mL) goo solution*
- resealable plastic bag

Directions:

1. Open the bag wide and place the glue and water at the bottom of the bag. (You may wish to add a few drops of food coloring for added dimension.)
2. Close the bag and squish water and glue together, keeping the mixture near the bottom until well blended.
3. Reopen the baggie and add the goo solution (recipe below).
4. Reseal the bag, pushing out excess air. Place in the center and allow students to squish.
5. A chemical reaction (change) begins to take place. After a minute or two, allow students to open the bag and pull out the goo.
4. Have students play and experiment with goo. It will eventually turn solid.

*Goo Solution

In a gallon container, mix 2 cups (500 mL) of dry borax (found in laundry soap aisle of a grocery store) in 1 gallon (4L) of boiling water. The borax will dissolve immediately. Seal the container and shake slightly. Cool the borax solution completely before you use it. It can be made up to 3 days ahead.

Hands-On Center Model

Activity:

Liquid Measurement

Skills:

Measuring various amounts of liquid

Objective:

To gain an understanding of liquid measurements and how they relate to one another

Materials:

- transparent measuring containers labeled cup, pint, quart, and gallon
- Liquid Measurements Discovery Chart (page 223), laminated
- pitcher
- water
- paper towels

Directions:

1. Locate the center near the sink. Place the materials in the center.

2. Allow students to follow the directions on the chart.

3. To clean up, have a student empty all the containers at the sink and use paper towels to dry them. Have the clean-up student wipe up any excess water that may have spilled at the center table.

4. Ask students to demonstrate what they have learned and share answers to the chart questions.

Liquid Measurements
Discovery Chart

Follow the directions in each numbered box and answer each of the questions.

1. Find the cup. Use it to fill the pint. How many cups are in a pint?

2. Find the pint. Use it to fill the quart. How many pints are in a quart?

3. Find the quart. Use it to fill the gallon. How many quarts are in a gallon?

4. Find the cup. Use it to fill the quart. How many cups are in a quart?

5. Find the pint. Use it to fill the gallon. How many pints are in a gallon?

6. Find the cup. Use it to fill the gallon. How many cups are in a gallon?

Drama Centers

Sometimes known as the home/dramatic play center, a Drama Center is a place in which students can engage in role-playing a variety of scenarios. Brainstorm with students to find what kinds of activities they would like to have available, and make a list so you can try new ones throughout the year while maintaining tried and true favorites, such as playing school, playing house, and staging plays. Encourage students to contribute as much as possible, such as student-made masks, headbands, paper bag costumes, or cardboard scenery and props or materials they bring from home to share.

Drama Centers (cont.)

Some Ideas

- puppet stage and puppets
- dishes and flatware
- costumes from different cultures
- unbreakable full-length mirror
- small sofa and chair
- small kitchen table and chairs
- play telephones
- dolls of different ethnic origins wearing traditional clothing
- cleaning equipment like scrub brushes and brooms
- cooking utensils like pots and pans
- dishtowels
- small rocking chair
- doll bed
- kitchen cabinets and sink
- refrigerator
- play food
- range, pot holders, and apron
- plastic fruits and vegetables

Inexpensive and Free Accessories

1. Save empty product boxes from grocery items, such as cereal and rice. If these are opened carefully, they can be glued back together and look as good as new.

2. Open cans, such as those containing soup and green beans, from the bottom instead of the top. Wash them thoroughly, and use as play food.

3. Ask parents to donate outgrown baby clothes that might fit the dolls in the center and old or broken costume jewelry.

4. Wash and bring in plastic butter tubs and similar items from home.

5. Bring in old magazines, catalogues, and greeting cards for students to use.

6. Look around the house for some old artificial flowers and a plastic vase to bring.

7. Have students create play food by drawing, coloring, cutting, and gluing paper food to cardboard boxes. You or a parent volunteer can carefully cut out the cardboard foods with a utility knife. Do not allow students to use the utility knife or to be nearby when it is being used by an adult.

Drama Center Model

Puppet theaters and productions are wonderfully suited to a drama center. Include the following supplies:

- old, clean socks
- fabric scraps
- fabric glue
- rubber bands

- buttons
- paper lunch sacks
- construction paper
- scissors

- glue
- crayons and markers
- craft sticks
- felt

Provide the materials for the students and let them create their own puppets. Have students use the Writing Center to work on scripts for the puppet show. They can work alone or in small teams to prepare and perform their scripts. Post the puppeteering tips on page 227 in the center. Allow students to rehearse at the actual "theater."

You may be lucky enough to have a wooden puppet stage. If not, simple ones can be easily created in the classroom.

1. Get a large appliance box. Cut an opening near the top of the box to serve as the stage for puppets.

2. Drape a sheet or blanket across one long edge of a table. Have the puppeteers work behind the table and move the puppets above it.

3. String a rope across a corner of the classroom and hang a sheet or blanket over it. Let the puppeteers work behind it, moving the puppets above it.

Tips for Puppeteers

1. Open the puppet's mouth for each syllable that you speak.

2. Keep the puppet's "feet" at or below the bottom of the opening so that the puppet does not appear to float in air.

3. Speak loudly. Remember, you are speaking behind a wall. Your voice needs to carry to the audience.

4. Be aware of your puppet at all times. Make your puppet "come alive"—and do not be afraid to exaggerate. Your audience is watching the puppet, and you want to keep the audience interested.

5. When using a sock puppet, you may wish to put a rubber band around the sock and your four fingers to help keep the puppet's mouth in place.

Theme and Seasonal Centers

A well-planned theme center can do a great deal of teaching for you. In a centers-based classroom, a teacher's role is different from that of a traditional classroom. Rather than standing in front of the class and imparting knowledge by talking and talking, teachers are guides who help students learn from their environment. As teachers move from center to center, they can interact with students to find out what each student is learning. This interaction is not an interrogation as much as a friendly conversation. For example, your questions may sound like this: What have you been working on this morning? Have you looked at any of the books? Which one did you like the best? Why? Which toy are you playing with? Did you know there is a toy to match this story? Do you know what it is called? What have you learned about manatees?

Using Science and Social Studies Books as Readers

When a center's theme is a science or social studies topic, there is economy of instruction. Even more time is saved if the "reader" is a science or social studies related book. Students are curious about most things in their world, and when offered a choice of reading for reading's sake or reading to discover more about a topic of interest, they will likely choose the book that reinforces and augments their learning about their chosen topic. Many young readers will enjoy books written by Eric Carle, and Tomie de Paola writes many nonfiction books that are suitable for and appreciated by older students.

Using Nonfiction Simplifies Evaluation

During a whole class session about a topic, create a fact chart. If you pencil in the initials of the student offering the fact, the chart can be used later for evaluation. Add difficult words to the topic word chart. Have students write nonfiction books by paraphrasing the chart and adding illustrations. Noticing the students who are only able to draw pictures and copy labels and those who may be more skilled at writing sentences and whole stories also provides you with an accurate evaluation of the skills and information being acquired by students. Use a read-aloud period to present related books that may be too difficult for the student to read alone.

Using Themes Can Be Easy

Themes can be carried over into as many subject areas as you have centers. Materials in a theme center should be portable. Students working in other centers may make short visits to the theme center to get materials. The following two rules must be maintained when students wish to borrow materials from a theme center.

1. Before borrowing any materials from a theme center, a student should make sure that the materials are not needed by students working in that center.

2. Borrowed materials must be returned to the theme center during clean-up time.

Theme and Seasonal Centers *(cont.)*

Here is how one theme may apply through the various curricular areas.

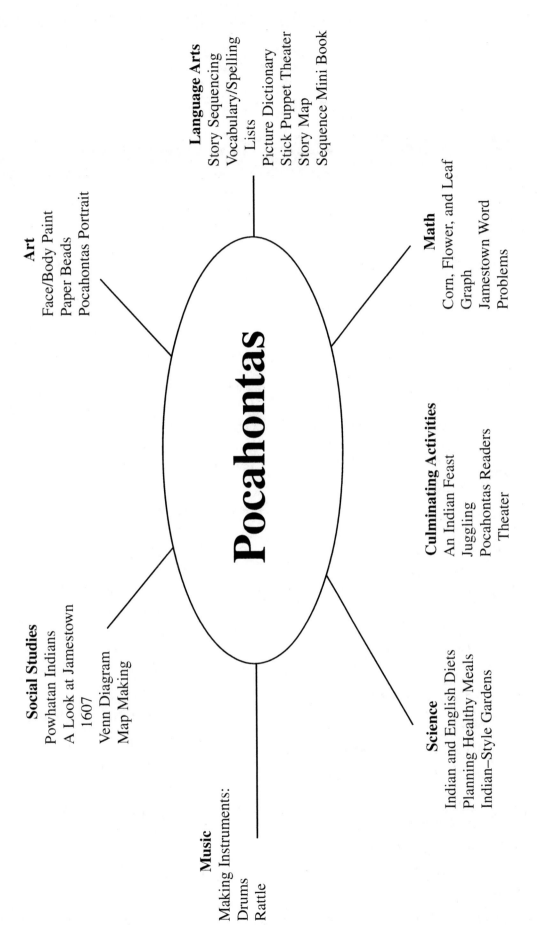

Language Arts
Story Sequencing
Vocabulary/Spelling
Lists
Picture Dictionary
Stick Puppet Theater
Story Map
Sequence Mini Book

Art
Face/Body Paint
Paper Beads
Pocahontas Portrait

Social Studies
Powhatan Indians
A Look at Jamestown 1607
Venn Diagram
Map Making

Music
Making Instruments:
Drums
Rattle

Science
Indian and English Diets
Planning Healthy Meals
Indian–Style Gardens

Culminating Activities
An Indian Feast
Juggling
Pocahontas Readers Theater

Math
Corn, Flower, and Leaf Graph
Jamestown Word Problems

Pocahontas

Theme and Seasonal Centers *(cont.)*

Theme Ideas

Science	Social Studies
Dinosaurs	Community
Rocks	Africa
Plants	Mexico
Water	The Arctic
Space	The Orient
Animal Classification	Native Americans
Magnetism, Energy, and Changes	Maps and Globes

Each of these themes can easily be made into cross-curricular experiences. First, students explore the theme center for a social studies experience. Extend the study into language arts by having students read books related to the theme. Continue the theme study by reading several fiction and nonfiction books aloud to the class. Be sure to include chapter books. Choices can be broad. If your social studies topic is the Arctic, look for books on similar topics, such as winter, people of the north, or polar bears.

More Theme Ideas

Fantasy	Cartoons and Comic Strips
Everyday Magic	Fairy Tales
Insects	Wild Things
Big and Little	State Symbols
That's Impossible (science)	Colors
Poetry	Circus
Nursery Rhymes	When Horses Were Cars (long ago)
Birds	Art and Beauty
Patriotism and Presidents	Nature (classify, compare, make patterns)
Animal Homes (habitats)	Let's Go (transportation, geography)
Friends	Down Under (Australia)
Food Around the World	Dr. Seuss
Seasons and Celebrations	Let's Play
Cultures of the World	
Family	

Theme and Seasonal Centers *(cont.)*

Making Connections

Students must be guided into recognizing and making connections between topics. A few simple adjustments in the curriculum can sometimes yield big dividends. For example, you may plan to teach three units, such as oceans, ecology, and rain forests. By sequencing these as a trio, you can emphasize relationships and generalizations. Pointing out the relationship among these three areas results in a much higher level of learning than having students study any of the topics in isolation.

Another strategy is to study relationships within the theme. Topics can be broad to include several related subtopics. For example, a thematic topic of "The Earth Long Ago" can include the study of dinosaurs, fossils, rocks, oil, ancient plant life, prehistory, etc. All these subjects are made more meaningful to the student by their connections to each other.

Oceans

Ecology

Rain Forest

Changing Themes

Leaving a specific theme center open for four to six weeks allows students to explore the theme in depth and gives you time to collect necessary materials and make assessments. You will probably want to change the theme center at least every grading period, if not every month.

Extending Themes Throughout the Curriculum

As each theme is completed, you may wish to retain some of the exhibits, books, and equipment. These can be incorporated into other centers. Perhaps a tank of fish and seashells that served as research material for report writing can be placed in the Art/Publishing Center to inspire students to write poetry. Shells are always popular for stimulating art projects, too.

Sometimes students enjoy outer-space themes so much they want to keep some of the space books in the classroom after the unit is finished. Simply move a few of their favorite books into a special space section in the Research Center or Library Center. The space shuttle and other space toys might be moved to the Block Center or Drama Center where students can use them to design a space city or stage a play.

Another way to recycle theme center materials is to create a temporary or special center. When float-and-sink materials have had their turn in a theme center, they can move to a Water/Sand Center. Change highly interactive centers such as those incorporating woodworking, sand, water, painting, music, etc., on a rotational basis to efficiently use the space in your classroom. These special centers are essential to the educational development of kindergarten children, and they also serve a purpose for older children. Hands-on, interactive learning certainly reinforces learning and very often teaches students much more than simple paper-and-pencil worksheet activities.

Theme and Seasonal Centers *(cont.)*

One way to organize classroom activities is to group them around the seasons and holidays. Here is a sample plan.

Month	Themes	Month	Themes
September	School starts Labor Day Rosh Hashanah Yom Kippur Fall	**March**	St. Patrick's Day Spring
October	Harvest Halloween Columbus Day Thanksgiving (Canada)	**April**	Easter (sometimes March) Earth Day
November	Thanksgiving Veteran's Day Remembrance Day (Canada)	**May**	Cinco de Mayo (Mexico) Mother's Day Memorial Day Victoria Day (Canada)
December	Christmas Hanukkah Winter Kwanzaa	**June**	Father's Day Quebec Day (Canada) Summer
January	New Year's Day Martin Luther King Jr.'s Birthday	**July**	Independence Day Canada Day (Canada) Bastille Day
February	Groundhog Day President's Day Valentine's Day Chinese New Year	**August**	Civic Holiday (Canada)

If you use such a plan, you will center reading and research books, art projects, story writing, and math content around the season or holidays. Encourage students to bring related things from home each month. The brainstorming webs on pages 233–238 may help you generate ideas and establish a plan for each month.

Theme and Seasonal Centers *(cont.)*

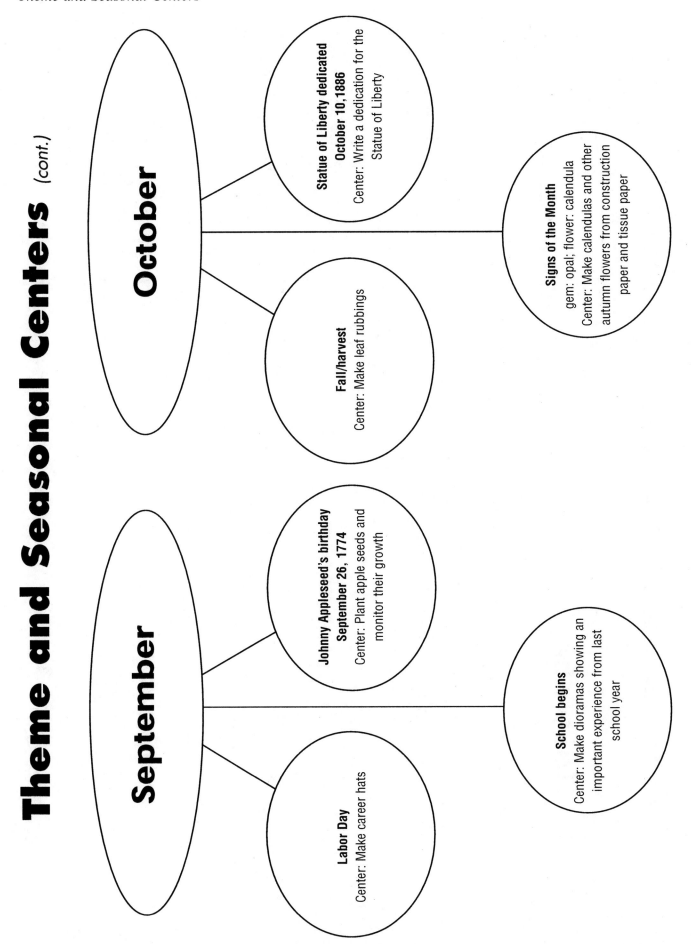

October

Statue of Liberty dedicated
October 10, 1886
Center: Write a dedication for the
Statue of Liberty

Signs of the Month
gem: opal; flower: calendula
Center: Make calendulas and other
autumn flowers from construction
paper and tissue paper

Fall/harvest
Center: Make leaf rubbings

September

**Johnny Appleseed's birthday
September 26, 1774**
Center: Plant apple seeds and
monitor their growth

School begins
Center: Make dioramas showing an
important experience from last
school year

Labor Day
Center: Make career hats

Theme and Seasonal Centers *(cont.)*

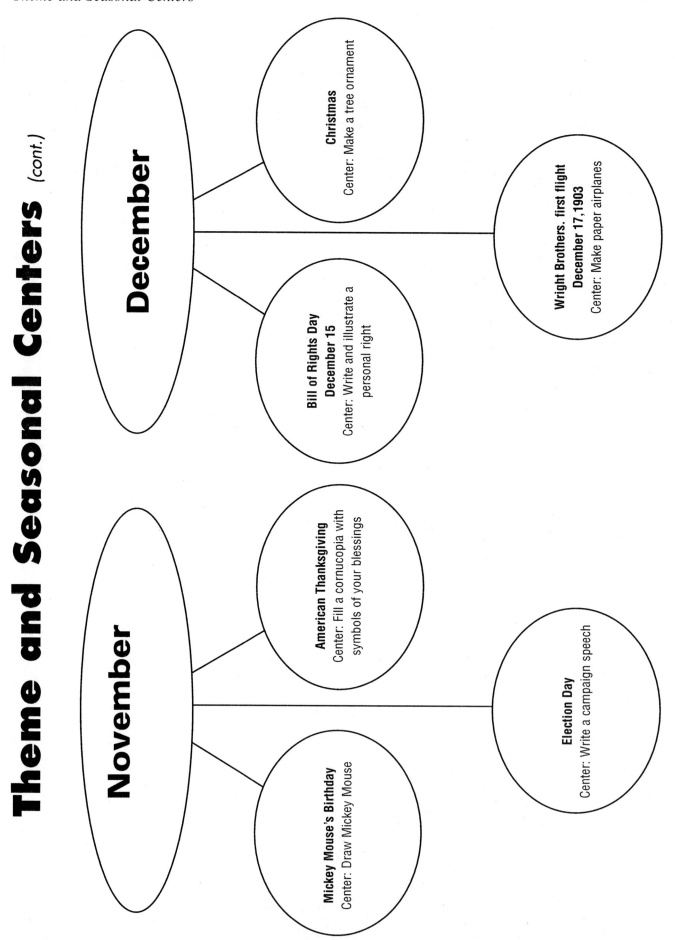

December

Christmas
Center: Make a tree ornament

Bill of Rights Day
December 15
Center: Write and illustrate a personal right

Wright Brothers. first flight
December 17, 1903
Center: Make paper airplanes

November

American Thanksgiving
Center: Fill a cornucopia with symbols of your blessings

Mickey Mouse's Birthday
Center: Draw Mickey Mouse

Election Day
Center: Write a campaign speech

Theme and Seasonal Centers *(cont.)*

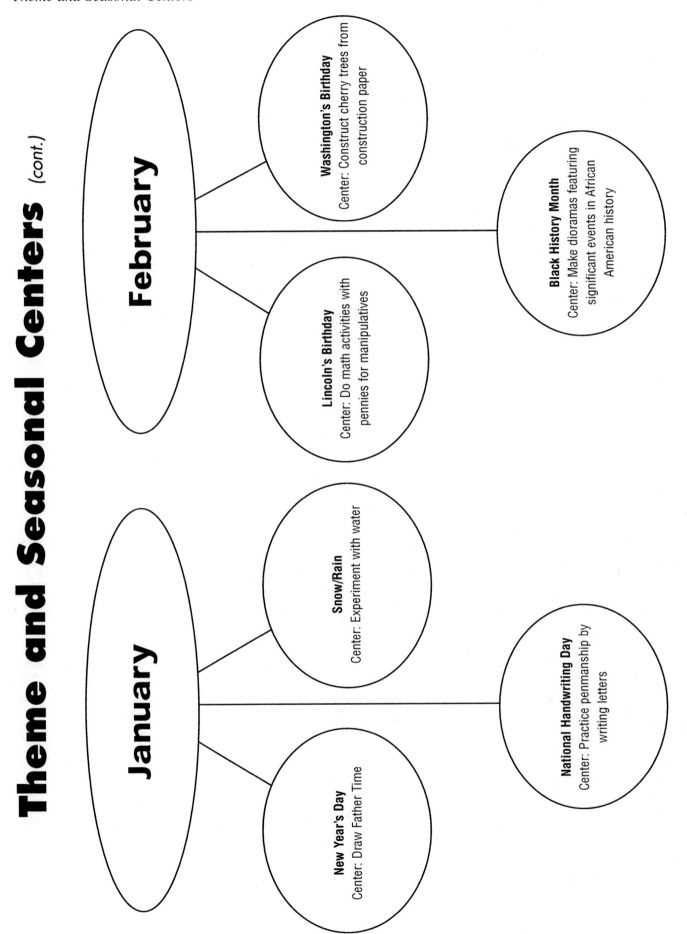

February

Washington's Birthday
Center: Construct cherry trees from construction paper

Lincoln's Birthday
Center: Do math activities with pennies for manipulatives

Black History Month
Center: Make dioramas featuring significant events in African American history

January

Snow/Rain
Center: Experiment with water

New Year's Day
Center: Draw Father Time

National Handwriting Day
Center: Practice penmanship by writing letters

Theme and Seasonal Centers *(cont.)*

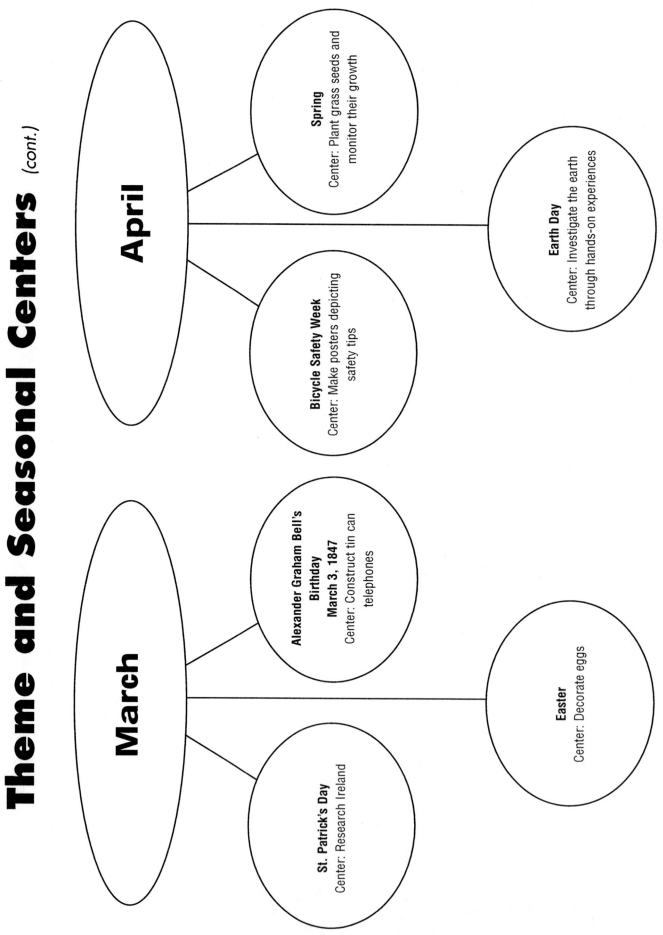

April

Spring

Center: Plant grass seeds and monitor their growth

Bicycle Safety Week

Center: Make posters depicting safety tips

Earth Day

Center: Investigate the earth through hands-on experiences

March

Alexander Graham Bell's Birthday
March 3, 1847

Center: Construct tin can telephones

St. Patrick's Day

Center: Research Ireland

Easter

Center: Decorate eggs

Theme and Seasonal Centers *(cont.)*

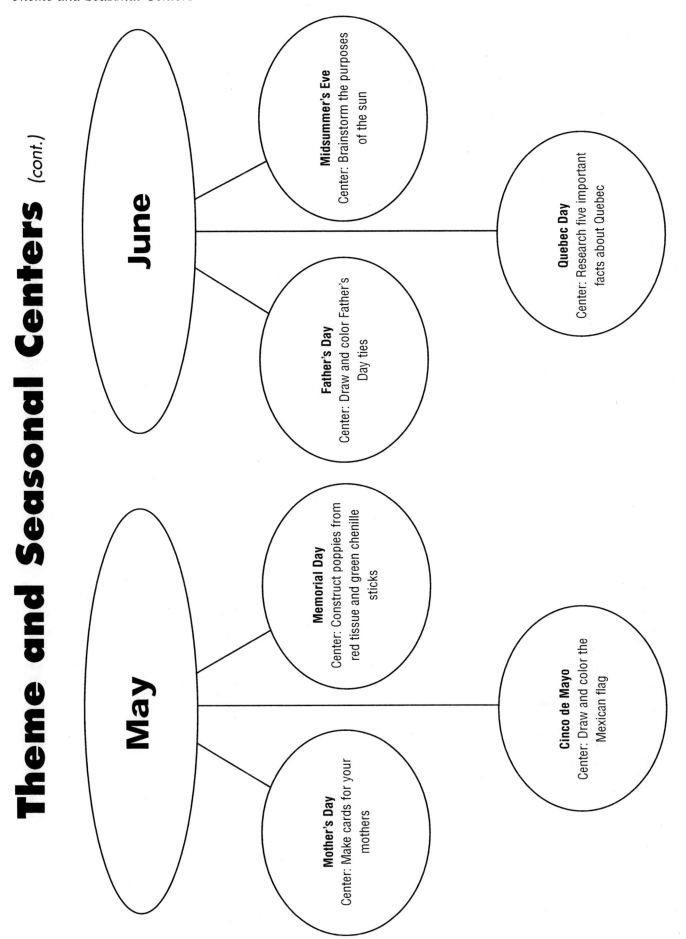

June

Midsummer's Eve
Center: Brainstorm the purposes of the sun

Father's Day
Center: Draw and color Father's Day ties

Quebec Day
Center: Research five important facts about Quebec

May

Memorial Day
Center: Construct poppies from red tissue and green chenille sticks

Mother's Day
Center: Make cards for your mothers

Cinco de Mayo
Center: Draw and color the Mexican flag

Theme and Seasonal Centers *(cont.)*

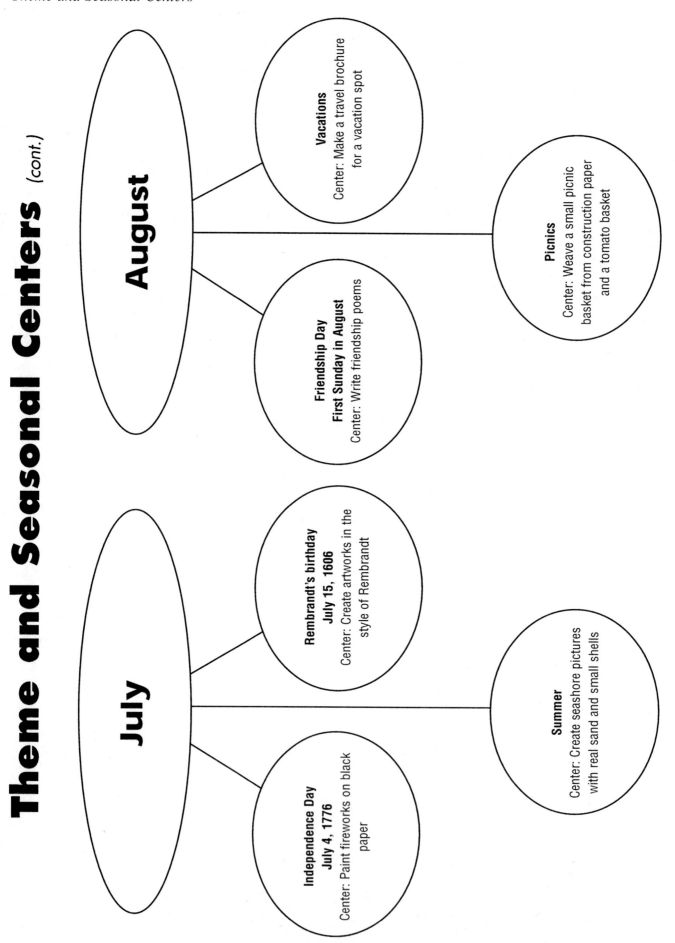

August

Vacations
Center: Make a travel brochure for a vacation spot

**Friendship Day
First Sunday in August**
Center: Write friendship poems

Picnics
Center: Weave a small picnic basket from construction paper and a tomato basket

July

**Rembrandt's birthday
July 15, 1606**
Center: Create artworks in the style of Rembrandt

**Independence Day
July 4, 1776**
Center: Paint fireworks on black paper

Summer
Center: Create seashore pictures with real sand and small shells

Theme and Seasonal Centers *(cont.)*

Special Events

One of the things that makes school special is that everyone gets to experience and learn about others from various heritages. School is one place where the similarities and differences among people in our American culture can be appreciated and celebrated.

Discover the family heritages of your students. Enlist parents' help whenever possible, and try to find books, games, and activities from these countries to share with the class. Plan time to share and celebrate the differences among all of you while also making connections to the similarities of everyone in the world.

You may wish to include other classes in your celebrations. Have each participating teacher choose, plan and lead a half-hour activity with groups of about 15 students. Rotate the students from all classes through the different "stations" during the day to create a special-events day.

Special Events Station Ideas

Author's Day

Inventor's Day

Veteran's Day

Special Person Day

Flag Day

Groundhog Day

Arbor Day

Memorial Day

Peace Day

Spring Festival

Make a spring mobile.

Brainstorm signs of spring.

Plant flower seeds.

Design a kite.

Make paper flowers.

Decorate flower pots.

Theme and Seasonal Centers *(cont.)*

Special Events—Station Suggestion Samples

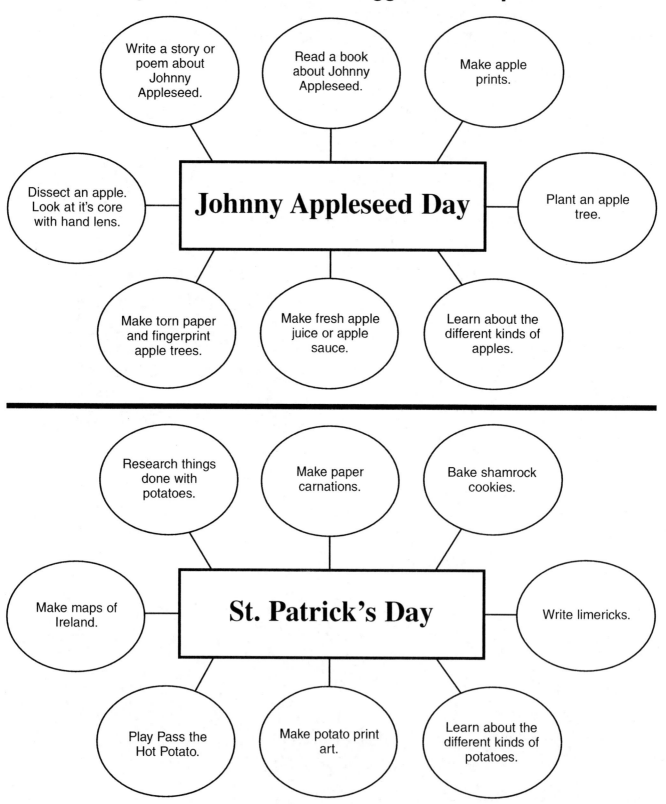

Tortilla Decorations

This is a fun activity that can be adapted to nearly any season, holiday, or theme center.

Materials:

- flour tortillas
- markers
- cookie cutters or patterns (page 242)
- scissors
- pencil
- hole puncher
- string or yarn

Directions:

1. Choose a cookie cutter and press it firmly onto a tortilla. If using a pattern, trace it onto the tortilla or draw your own shape onto the tortilla. Cut it out with scissors.

2. Decorate the shape with markers.

3. Punch a hole in the top of the shape.

4. Let the tortilla dry.

5. Use string or yarn to hang the shapes in a display or on mobiles.

Patterns

tree

leaf

sun

egg

heart

snowman

witch

flower

Centers Signs and Markers

To identify your centers, reproduce the signs in this section onto sturdy paper, color them, laminate them, and place them at the appropriate center.

- Tape them to the wall.

- Punch a hole on either side and make a yarn hanger to hook on a nail or hook.

- Punch a hole in the top and hang the sign on a nail.

- Make a clothespin stand for the sign.

  1. Cut a tennis ball in half with a utility knife or scissors.

  2. Line both halves with plastic wrap.

  3. Fill the halves with plaster of Paris.

  4. Place a paper towel roll tube into each ball, pressing it gently into the plaster of Paris and ensuring that the tube remains straight. Allow the plaster to dry thoroughly.

  5. Peel away the tennis ball and plastic wrap. (You may wish to cut or scrape part of the rounded part off to stabilize the plaster bases.)

  6. Paint the plaster, the tube, and two clothespins with tempera paint. Allow to dry.

  7. Use the clothespins to attach the sign to the tube.

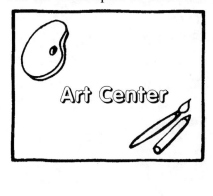

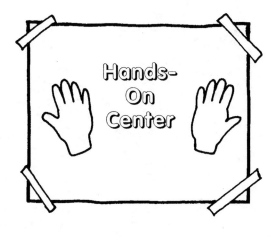

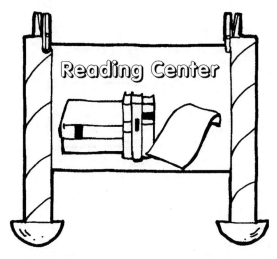

Centers Signs and Markers (cont.)

Centers Signs and Markers (cont.)

Centers Signs and Markers *(cont.)*

Centers Signs and Markers *(cont.)*

Centers Signs and Markers (cont.)

Centers Signs and Markers (cont.)

Centers Signs and Markers (cont.)

Social Studies Center

Centers Signs and Markers (cont.)

Centers Signs and Markers *(cont.)*

Centers Signs and Markers *(cont.)*

Centers Signs and Markers (cont.)

Centers Signs and Markers (cont.)

Hands-On Center

Centers Signs and Markers (cont.)

Drama Center

Centers Signs and Markers (cont.)

Centers Signs and Markers *(cont.)*

Fill in this sign for any other center you might have.

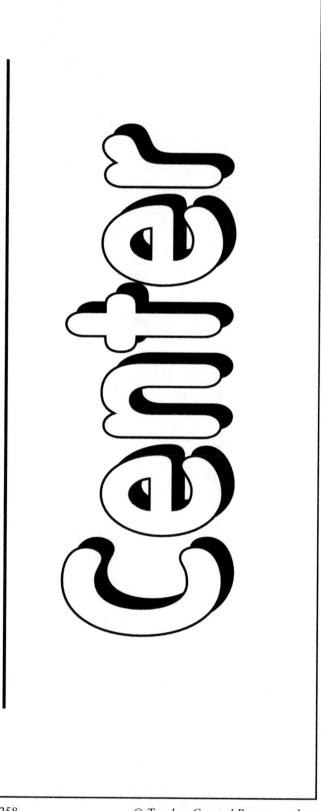

Centers Signs and Markers *(cont.)*

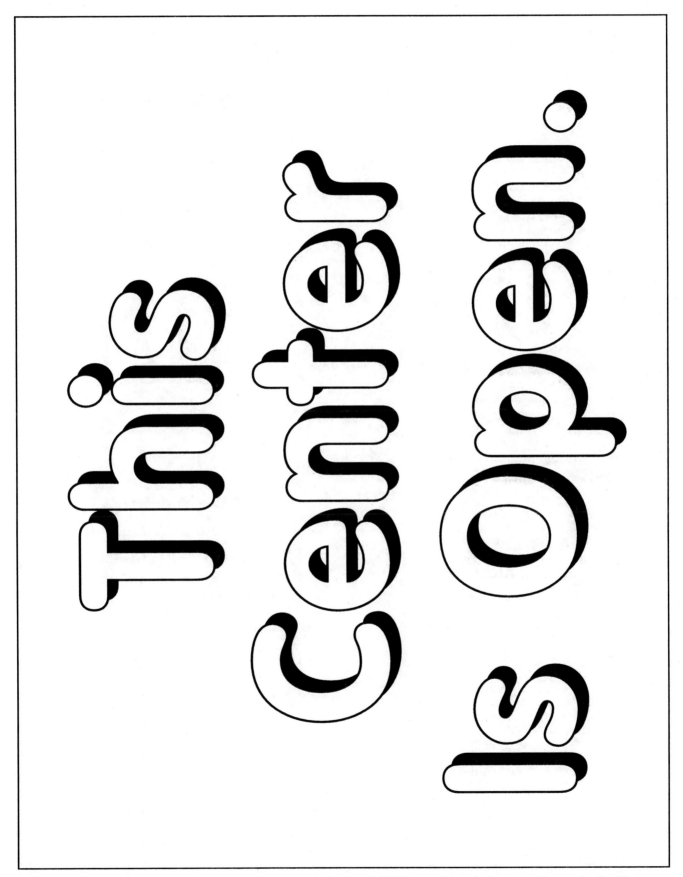

Centers Signs and Markers *(cont.)*

Centers Signs and Markers *(cont.)*

Listening Center

Reading Center

Library Center

Centers Signs and Markers *(cont.)*

Writing Center

Math Center

Science Center

Centers Signs and Markers *(cont.)*

Social Studies Center

Research Center

Computer Center

Centers Signs and Markers *(cont.)*

Art Center

Puzzles and Games Center

Hands-On Center

Centers Signs and Markers *(cont.)*

Drama Center

About Me Center

_____ Center

Directions for Students

Some form of symbolic directions for students will make the centers easier to use even if you orally explain a center. These symbols will be especially helpful for students who are not yet reading or who have limited English proficiency.

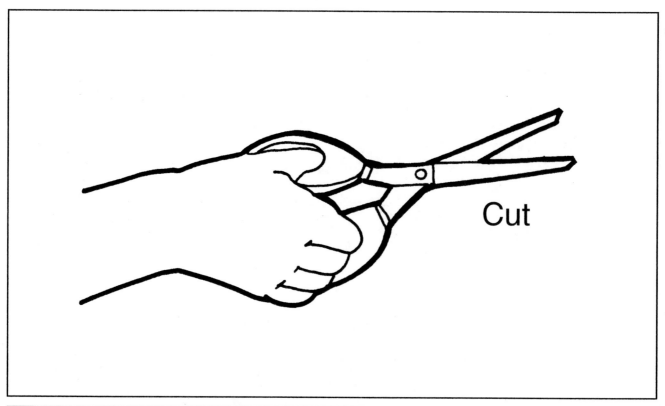

Cut

Paste

Directions for Students *(cont.)*

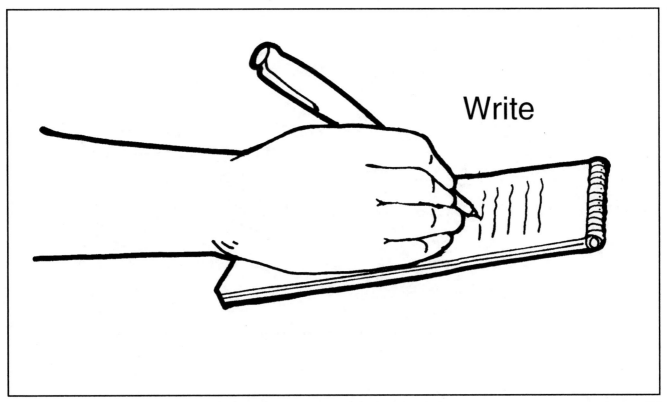

Write

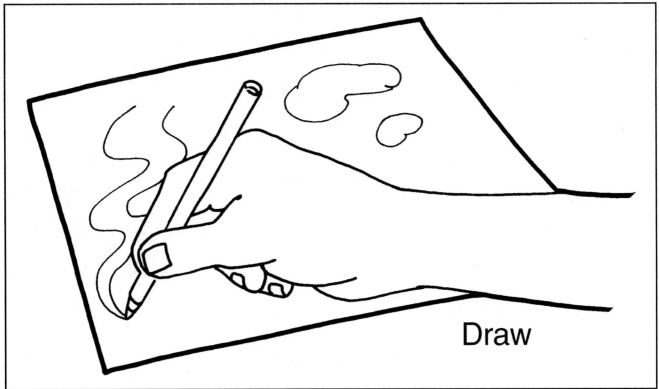

Draw

Directions for Students *(cont.)*

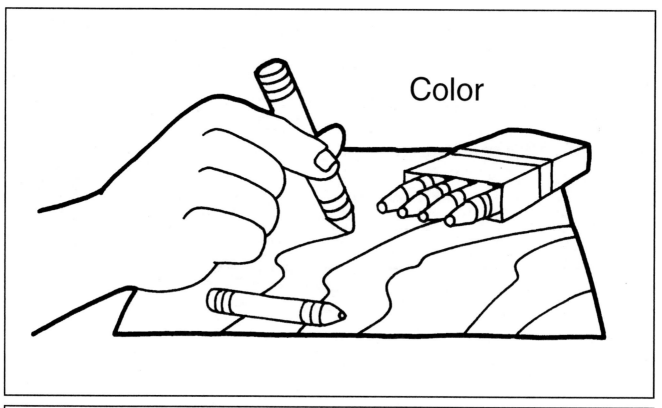

Color

Read

Assessment and Contracts

Here are some suggestions to help you evaluate and assess student work from learning centers.

- Keep a box or basket where students can place finished center work. At the end of each day, take time to share the work in the box with the class. Make positive comments about each piece of work along with constructive suggestions (if necessary). Give the owner an opportunity to comment on his or her work if he or she wishes to. This sharing time is a good motivational and informative tool.

- Make a monthly calendar for each student. Store it in a three-ring binder at the centers. Record information in the appropriate spaces.

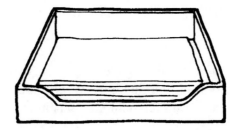

- Keep a file box with students' names listed alphabetically on index cards. Record notes and activities completed on the cards.

- Checklists are fast and easy to use. See the samples and blank forms on pages 271–274.

- Use the tips and forms on pages 275–281 to keep anecdotal records of student work.

- Pages 282–284 offer rubric guides to be used for assessment based on the anecdotal records.

- Let students self-evaluate; keep their evaluations in their files. Two useful forms can be found on pages 285–286.

- Sample contracts you may wish to use to document the completion of center work are on pages 287–291. The extent to which students have honored their contracts can also be a useful tool in assessment.

Observation-Based Assessment

Observation-based assessment is a new name for something teachers have been doing for years. You have always carefully observed your students, while making mental and written notes about their progress. However, you may not have always considered this activity as an assessment. There are two basic types of observations you can make: objective and interpretive. When being objective, you record what you see as if you were a camera. Checklists are an objective form of assessment. Anecdotal records, on the other hand, can be either objective or interpretive. The interpretive style of assessment goes beyond mere recording and involves your actually evaluating and commenting on the notes you have taken. Learn to trust and use your judgment!

Using Checklists

Checklists serve only as an indication of whether something existed (happened) or not as seen by an observer. With a checklist there is no need to judge how well or poorly something was done. You may wish to create your own checklists with your personal assessment criteria for students.

Using Anecdotal Records

Anecdotal records are carefully documented notes of certain events, behaviors, and skills. When anecdotal records are put together, they tell an ongoing story about a student's delays and progress. At the beginning of the year, it may be necessary to make more general entries as you start the process of becoming familiar with your students. As you get to know your students, your entries may become more specific, or the type of entry may change. A simple way to record anecdotal records involves using several copies of a recording form and a notebook. You may choose to have a form for each individual student or one form you can use for the whole class. Use them to note observations you make of students throughout the course of the school day.

Using a Rubric

A rubric is a set of criteria students see prior to engaging in a task. A rubric can be established for a single task or for several tasks. A rubric identifies what exactly you expect to see students accomplish along several points on a scale. Each score on the rubric is matched to an example of a response. By viewing established criteria prior to the activity, students know what is expected of them in order to receive a specific score.

Using Student Self-Evaluation

Students can become involved in the assessment process by reflecting on certain assignments. Self-evaluation makes students aware of their own learning, progress, and growth throughout the school year. You can introduce students to the self-evaluation process by having them complete reflections forms. If they are unable to complete a form, you or parents can sit down with the students and ask them to talk about their performance on an assignment as you transcribe it.

Do not expect students to jump right into self-evaluation without training them. Students are used to doing classroom work and then waiting for the teacher to return it with a grade. Evaluating one's own work is not easy, and taking responsibility for it is certainly a challenge. It will take a while for students to begin to trust their own judgment, so be patient.

Sample Checklist—A

Student Name: *Peter Hokussai*

Curriculum Area: Writing *(One writing assignment per month; enter date completed; list piece by title and type.)*

9/21	"Here I Go"	Essay/Reflection
10/28	"Spooks"	Narrative with dialogue
11/20	"Thankful"	Poem
12/15	"Shop Early"	Persuasive

Teacher/Student Conferences   *(Enter dates.)*

9/30   10/31   11/25

Other Student Requirements

- ☑ List of Books Read
- ☑ Interest Inventory
- ☑ Reflections on Writing
- ☐
- ☐

Teacher Additions

- ☑ Anecdotal Records
- ☑ Running Records
- ☑ Scoring Rubric and Score
- ☐
- ☐

Checklist—A

Student Name: _____

Curriculum Area:

(One writing assignment per month; enter date completed; list piece by title and type.)

_____   _____

_____   _____

_____   _____

_____   _____

_____   _____

_____   _____

_____   _____

Teacher/Student Conferences   *(Enter dates.)*

_____   _____   _____   _____

Other Student Requirements   ## Teacher Additions

☐ List of Books Read   ☐ Anecdotal Records

☐ Interest Inventory   ☐ Running Records

☐ Reflections on Writing   ☐ Scoring Rubric and Score

☐   ☐

☐   ☐

Sample Checklist—B

Student's Name: *Paloma Sanchez*

Center: *Dinosaurs* **Date:** *10/31*

- ✔ Reading *list of books read*
- ✔ Writing *"Dilly, the Dino"*
- ✔ Math *Dinosaur word problems*
- ✔ Social Studies *Map of inland seas*
- ✔ Science *Album of dinosaur pictures, labeled*
- ✔ Art *Work on class dinosaur mural*
- ✔ Other *Culminating activity—party invitation*
- ____ Other _____

Center: _____ **Date:** _____

- _____ Reading _____
- _____ Writing _____
- _____ Math _____
- _____ Social Studies _____
- _____ Science _____
- _____ Art _____
- _____ Other _____
- _____ Other _____

Center: _____ **Date:** _____

- _____ Reading _____
- _____ Writing _____
- _____ Math _____
- _____ Social Studies _____
- _____ Science _____
- _____ Art _____
- _____ Other _____
- _____ Other _____

Checklist—B

Student's Name: _____

Center: **Date:**

_____ Reading _____
_____ Writing _____
_____ Math _____
_____ Social Studies _____
_____ Science _____
_____ Art _____
_____ Other _____
_____ Other _____

Center: **Date:**

_____ Reading _____
_____ Writing _____
_____ Math _____
_____ Social Studies _____
_____ Science _____
_____ Art _____
_____ Other _____
_____ Other _____

Center: **Date:**

_____ Reading _____
_____ Writing _____
_____ Math _____
_____ Social Studies _____
_____ Science _____
_____ Art _____
_____ Other _____
_____ Other _____

Anecdotal Records

Keeping anecdotal notes about student achievement is not a new method of record keeping. What is changing is the way anecdotal records are being used. The most common method of reporting student progress has been the use of letter or numerical grades. Today, the emphasis on using anecdotal records and checklists is growing.

Anecdotal notes offer more specific and useful information than grades. They also invite more parent participation. As parents become more aware of the specific strengths and weaknesses of their children as students, they may be encouraged to become more and more involved with their children's education.

How to Keep Anecdotal Records

You may need training and practice to keep good anecdotal records. The easiest way to begin is to pretend to be a video camera. A video camera records everything it focuses on and makes no judgment. It is factually accurate and specific. Here are some examples of anecdotal notes.

> **Poor:** Johnny is a good reader.
> **Better:** Johnny is reading with speed and fluency. He often chooses reading as an elective activity.

> **Poor:** Betty is very shy.
> **Better:** Betty is very quiet in class.

> **Poor:** Andre is struggling with math.
> **Better:** Andre is continuing to work on addition facts with sums of 5 or less.

> **Poor:** Norma is a good math student.
> **Better:** Norma has learned how to count by 5s and to count backwards.

> **Poor:** Judy is a sweet little girl.
> **Better:** Judy follows class rules.

> **Poor:** Brian is all boy.
> **Better:** Brian commits an occasional infraction of class rules.

Avoiding Problems

It is best to phrase comments about students in a positive manner so you don't alienate parents and cause problems by putting them on the defensive about their child. Sometimes it can be difficult to report accurately to parents without offending them. At the same time, you need to give a clear picture of the child's progress. Be as objective as possible. Do not compare one student with other students. During a conference, be sure to compare the student's work with her or his previous work. Quantitative reports are also very effective in anecdotal reports. Example: This is a list of the books your child has read this year.

Individual Anecdotal Record— Sample

Here is an example of how to keep an individual record of observed behaviors. Prepare one page for each student and file them in alphabetical order in a three-ring binder for easy access. When the page is filled, place it in the student's portfolio and begin a new page. Reproduce and use any of the blank forms on pages 277-279.

Individual Anecdotal Record

Name *Marcie Wallace*

Date	Comment
3/15/96	*Having trouble following directions while working on her own. We reviewed the importance of directions and where they can be found at each center.*
3/31/96	*Marcie followed almost all directions during Centers' Time with minimal prompting from me.*
4/3/96	*Marcie has taken full responsibility for reading and following center directions. She has helped John and Kim to do the same.*

Individual Anecdotal Record—A

Individual Anecdotal Record

Name _____

Date	Comment

Individual Anecdotal Record—B

✍ Anecdotal Record ✍

Date _____

Student's Name _____

Subject _____

Instructional Situation _____

Instructional Task _____

Behavior Observed _____

_____

_____

_____

_____

_____

_____

_____

Behavior Important Because _____

_____

_____

_____

_____

_____

_____

Individual Anecdotal Record—C

Anecdotal Record

Name _____ Date _____ Location _____ Time _____ _____ **Intellectual**　　**Social** **Emotional**　　**Physical**	Name _____ Date _____ Location _____ Time _____ _____ **Intellectual**　　**Social** **Emotional**　　**Physical**
Name _____ Date _____ Location _____ Time _____ _____ **Intellectual**　　**Social** **Emotional**　　**Physical**	Name _____ Date _____ Location _____ Time _____ _____ **Intellectual**　　**Social** **Emotional**　　**Physical**

Class Anecdotal Record— Sample

Here is an example of how to keep a classroom record of observed behaviors. Write comments daily and transfer them, with elaboration, to individual student records at the end of the day. File them in chronological order in a three-ring binder for easy access. Reproduce and use the blank form on page 281.

Record of Observed Behaviors

Date	Student's Name	Comment
3/31/96	Paul L.	Holding up pretty well in spite of Halloween! Wrote a great scary story
3/31/96	Marcie W.	Made several positive comments to the others working at her center - "I like that." and "What a nice story."
4/3/96	Joe S.	Needs help reading his new book - find parent helper.
4/3/96	Marcie W.	Continues to be positive and helpful. Shared today in oral language.

Class Anecdotal Record

Record of Observed Behaviors

Date	Student's Name	Comment

General Rubric Criteria Levels

6 Exemplary performance.

5 Acceptable performance.

4 Adequate performance, but doesn't quite meet criteria for acceptable work.

3 Inadequate performance, but showed great effort to complete the task.

2 Unacceptable performance, but showed good effort to complete the task.

1 Unacceptable performance, and showed little effort to complete the task.

0 Made no effort to participate, respond, or complete the task.

Generalized Task Rubric

Use this model to develop your own generalized task rubric. Begin by completing the criteria for levels 5 and 2.

Generalized Task Rubric

6

5

4

3

2

1

0

Rubric Evaluation

Name _____

Area Evaluated:

Guidelines Used:

Task: **Observational Scale**

Date/Comments	0	1	2	3	4	5	6
Date/Comments							
Date/Comments							
Date/Comments							

© *Teacher Created Resources, Inc.*

Self-Evaluation—A

Name: _____

_____

Task: _____

_____

1. How do you feel about this task? (Circle one.)

happy   **not sure**   **sad**

2. What did you do best on this task?

_____

_____

_____

3. What could you improve on this task?

_____

_____

_____

_____

_____

Self-Evaluation—B

Name: _____

Assignment: _____

1. How do you feel about this assignment? _____

   _____

   _____

   _____

   _____

   _____

   _____

2. What did you do best on this assignment? _____

   _____

   _____

   _____

   _____

   _____

   _____

3. If you were to do this assignment again, what would you do differently?_____

   _____

   _____

   _____

   _____

   _____

Centers Contract

Bubble Colors
Monday (red)
Tuesday (orange)
Wednesday (yellow)
Thursday (green)
Friday (blue)

Name_____ Start Date _____

▭	Number _____ Meet with Teacher _____	◯
☆		◯ ◯
✚		◯ ◯
⇨		◯ ◯
◯		◯ ◯
♡		◯ ◯
△		◯ ◯
▯		◯ ◯
▢		◯ ◯
⬡		◯ ◯
◇		◯ ◯
▢		◯ ◯

Teacher's Comments	Parent's Comments
	Please sign and return_____

Expectations Contract

This is the _____ Center. I understand that to complete this center's activities satisfactorily I am expected to:

Students' Signatures

_____   _____

_____   _____

_____   _____

_____   _____

_____   _____

_____   _____

_____   _____

_____   _____

_____   _____

_____   _____

_____   _____

_____   _____

_____   _____

Contract—Grades 1-3

Agreement between the teacher and student can be reached orally. Specific assignments are written in by the teacher during a conference with the student.

CONTRACT

I have just finished _____

_____.

The next thing I will do in _____

is _____

_____.

I will have this done by my next conference on _____

_____.

_____
Student

_____
Date

Contract—Grades 4-6

Use teacher/student conference time to its best advantage by having the student make a definite commitment to his or her next steps in the learning process.

CONTRACT

Having just completed _____

_____ ,

my next steps in the area of _____

are _____

_____

_____

_____ .

I agree to complete these assignments by _____

which is the date of my next conference.

_____

Student

_____

Date

Computer Contract

Computer Contract

I, _____, promise to treat computers with respect. I will follow all computer rules. I promise to:

1. Have clean hands when using the computer.
2. Touch the computer in a gentle way.
3. Not eat or drink at the computer.
4. Use my indoor voice when I use the computer.

I promise to be a respectful computer student.

_____   _____
Student   Date

Accommodating Students with Special Needs

The number of attention deficit disorder, attention deficit hyperactivity disorder, fetal alcohol syndrome, and inclusion students is rising dramatically, and teachers must accommodate the needs of these students as well as their other students. In addition, issues of English language acquisition and development contribute to classroom diversity. For most of these special needs students, a learning center environment meets individual needs far better than a traditional setting. Learning centers can be tailored to individual needs, limited attention spans, and specific language needs.

Some students, particularly those with learning disabilities or attention deficit disorder, can have difficulty in a less structured environment (Hallahan & Kauffman, 1994)* and are sometimes more successful in settings with greater structure and less stimuli. You may wish to provide a special cubicle for these students and encourage them to complete their learning center activities at the cubicle location. It is important they choose to do their work in this special location and that they understand why it will help them learn. It is easy to create such cubicles out of cardboard boxes or as individual desk carrels.

The freedom and independence provided by a learning center based classroom can at times overwhelm all students and lead to problems. For those students, you may wish to incorporate some or all of these suggestions:

- Individualize the student's work. Make daily goals with the student and meet regularly throughout the day to monitor and evaluate progress.

- Assign the student a buddy to work with at all of the centers.

- Work with the student and his or her parent(s) to develop a behavior contract. Record daily behavior and progress on a card and send it home for a parent to sign and return each day.

- As a last resort, do not allow the students to participate in the centers until the improper behavior is modified. Give him or her the assignments to do at a desk and do not allow movement around the room. Students so restricted usually miss the freedom that learning centers allow and change their behavior quickly.

* Hallahan, D.P. and Kauggman, J.M. (1994). *Exceptional Children*. Needham Heights, MA: Allyn & Bacon.

What Learning Centers Are

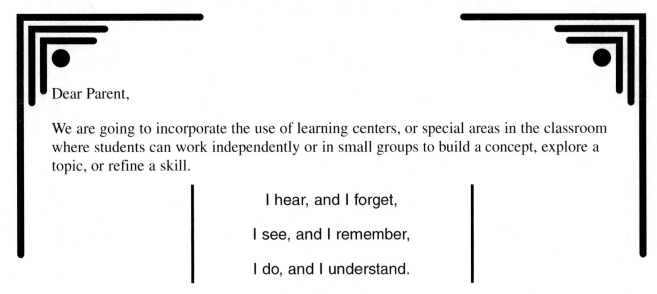

Dear Parent,

We are going to incorporate the use of learning centers, or special areas in the classroom where students can work independently or in small groups to build a concept, explore a topic, or refine a skill.

> I hear, and I forget,
>
> I see, and I remember,
>
> I do, and I understand.

Learning centers support this Chinese proverb, as well as John Dewey's philosophy that learning is doing. In a learning centers based classroom, the teacher becomes a facilitator and observer, while students learn through active participation and independence rather than strictly teacher-directed activities.

A learning center can be as simple as a magnet lying on a table or as complex as an entire discovery lesson with directions and questions for analysis. Centers can have specific learning objectives for each student or simply provide students with opportunities for exploration and inquiry. Learning centers allow students to work creatively, independently, and in small groups; they are based on the premise that students need and deserve the freedom to explore and inquire in a manner that is comfortable for them.

In order for students to construct knowledge that is meaningful to them, most successful centers focus on reinforcement or enrichment. That is, they do not attempt to introduce new concepts or information. Rather, they serve to review and provide additional opportunities for enrichment by supporting what is being taught in the classroom. They also have a variety of activities that accommodate different learning styles and interests.

If you have any questions about learning centers, I will be happy to discuss them with you at any time.

Best wishes,

_____
       Teacher

Why We Are Using Learning Centers

Dear Parent,

As we begin our use of learning centers in the classroom, I want to provide you with some of the rationale behind them.

The advantages of learning centers are many! Teachers who have made the transition from traditional teacher-directed activities to student-initiated learning centers are ecstatic over the results. The following benefits are convincing many teachers to join in:

- Student Autonomy
- Cooperative Learning
- Concrete Experiences
- Individualization
- Peer Tutoring
- Better Use of Resources

The use of learning centers promotes the fact that students are capable of working independently and cooperatively without the teacher's direct involvement. Rather than making the teacher the primary resource for knowledge, learning centers give ownership and autonomy to the students. They encourage individuality, facilitate learning styles and preferences, and accommodate varied rates of learning.

As autonomous learners, students learn to self-pace and self-evaluate. While these are not easy strategies to learn, they are vital for success. Students enjoy the freedom to choose, plan projects, and revise time lines, if needed. Often centers are student-initiated projects. Meeting regularly with the teacher, students must set and reach goals in a manner congruent with that of the teacher's expectations.

If you have any questions about learning centers, I will be happy to discuss them with you at any time.

Best wishes,

_____

    Teacher

Student Supplies

Dear Parent,

As part of our study of _____, we will be _____

_____. Please have your child bring

_____

_____

_____

_____to school

by _____.

If you are willing also to supply any of the items listed below, please send them to school
with your child.

_____

_____

_____

_____

Thank you for your support.

Yours truly,

_____
          Teacher

Capitalizing on Human Resources

Need

The need for additional assistance in any classroom is paramount. Teachers need help, whether it be working with a group of students, putting up a display board, or preparing a handout. Demands on parents' time often limit their ability to volunteer in their children's classroom, and limited funds have decreased the availability of paid assistants.

Strategies

What can you do to recruit and train parent or other adult volunteers, paid instructional assistants, tutors, or student helpers? Strategies include sending frequent requests for help to parents and other adults (page 297), calling and accepting any time a parent or other adult is available to help, training volunteers during lunch recess, teaming with teachers to share assistant time, creative financing through alternative means, and working with teachers at other grade levels to establish beneficial tutor schedules, guidelines, and training. Be flexible with daily schedules and try to capitalize on whatever is possible.

Communication

Keeping positive and open lines of communication with parents will always be an important facet of good teaching. Most parents are concerned about their children's education, whether or not they are able to participate actively in the daily classroom routine. The team effort between parents and teachers can be a terrific experience and great benefit to both parties, but the greatest winners are the students.

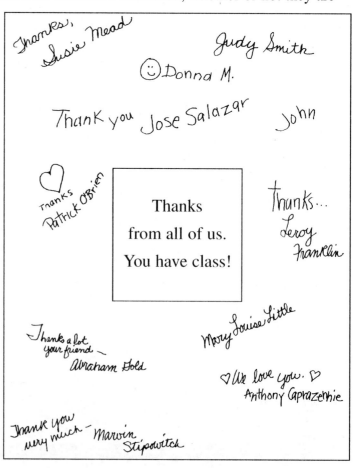

Record Keeping

Reproduce and use pages 298–299 to recruit volunteers, maintain a record of their work, and to facilitate their making anecdotal observations.

Thanking Your Volunteers

Make a copy of page 300 and have students write their names around the border. Then make another copy to send as a thank you to your classroom volunteers.

Request for Help

Date _____,

Dear _____,

In order to make our classroom programs as successful as they possibly can be, we need the help of volunteers. Are you willing to offer at least one hour a week to help? The times I most need volunteer assistance are:

_____

_____

_____

_____

_____

_____

Please mark the time that is best for you and return this form to me by

_____.

Thank you!

Best wishes,

_____
     Teacher

Please help us!

Volunteer Sign-In Sheet

Please record the information in the chart. Thank you so much for your help.

Name	Time In	Time Out	Task

Volunteer's Anecdotal Record

While you are working with the students, please make note of any behaviors or experiences that you wish to call to my attention. Thank you.

Volunteer's Name _____   Date _____

Student's Name _____
Observation:

Student's Name _____
Observation:

Student's Name _____
Observation:

Student's Name _____
Observation:

Thank You!

(see page 296)

> Thanks
>
> from all of us.
>
> You have class!

Clip Art

Clip Art *(cont.)*

Clip Art *(cont.)*

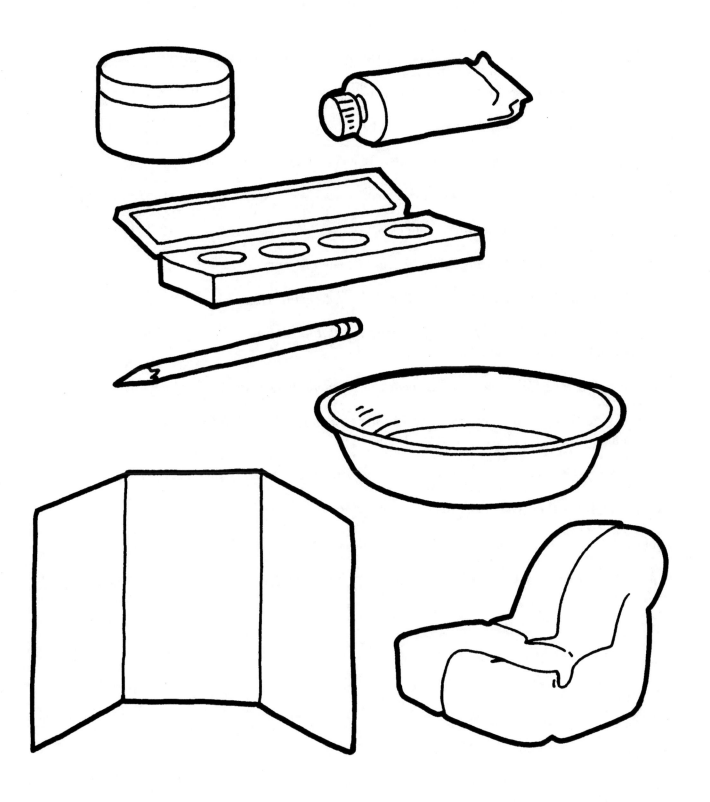

Bibliography

Glasser, W. Quality school: *Managing Students Without Coercion.* Harper & Row, 1990.

Goodlad, J.I. and J. Oakes. *We Must Offer Equal Access to Knowledge.* Educational Leadership, February 1988: 8, 16-22.

Graves, D.H. and B.S. Sunstein, B.S. (Eds.). *Portfolio Portraits.* Heinemann, 1992.

Hallahan, D.P.and J.M Kauffman,. *Exceptional Children.* Allyn & Bacon, 1994.

Jasmine, G. *Early Childhood Assessment.* Teacher Created Resources, 1995.

Jasmine, J. *Portfolios and Other Assessments.* Teacher Created Resources, 1993.

Kantrowitz, B. and P. Wingert, *"How Kids Learn"* Newsweek, April 17, 1989, 50-57.

Lazear, D. *Seven Ways of Teaching.* Skylight, 1991.

McClay, J.L. *The Multi-Age Classroom.* Teacher Created Resources, 1996.

Opitz, M.F. *Learning Centers: Getting Them Started, Keeping Them Going.* Scholastic, 1994.

Pattillo, J., and E. Vaughan, E. *Learning Centers for child-centered classrooms.* National Education Association of the United States, 1992.

Petreshene, S.S. *The Complete Guide to Learning Centers.* Pendragon House, Inc., 1978.

Poppe, C.A. and N.A. Van Matre. Science *Learning Centers for the Primary Grades.* The Center for Applied Research in Education, Inc., 1985.

Routman, R. Invitations: *Changing as Teachers and Learners K-12.* Heinemann, 1991.

Ryan, C.D. *Authentic Assessment.* Teacher Created Resources, 1994.

Thomas, J.I. *Learning centers: Opening Up the classroom.* Holbrook Press, 1975.

Wallace, A.H. *Learning Centers Through the Year.* Teacher Created Resources, 1993.